Avoiding the
Networking Disconnect

Avoiding the Networking Disconnect

THE THREE R'S TO RECONNECT

Ivan Misner, Ph.D. and Brennan Scanlon

Givers Gain® is a registered trademark of BNI®
Creating Referrals for Life® is a registered trademark of the Referral Institute®
VCP® is a registered trademark of the Referral Institute®
ISBN: 150789032X
ISBN 13: 9781507890325
Library of Congress Control Number: 2015907003
CreateSpace Independent Publishing Platform
North Charleston, South Carolina
Published in Austin, Texas by En Passant

Table of Contents

Acknowledgments

We would like to thank all of the wonderful people who helped make this book a reality: Christine Luken (The Word Nerd) for the brilliant editing work; Doug Silva of Midnite Graphics for the perfect cover and layout; our BNI directors and members, who gave us the delightful stories enclosed in this book; and finally, our families, who have given us the encouragement and the time to continue sharing our ideas with the world.

Dedication

Brennan

I dedicate this book to my father, Geoffrey L. Scanlon. No one has believed in my professional abilities more than he has, and no one has coached and mentored me more, either. Clarence B. Kelland once wrote, "My father did not teach me how to live; he lived and let me watch him do it." Geof Scanlon came up at a tough time; it was the 1940s and 1950s in Covington, Kentucky. The oldest of six children, he often found himself in the fatherly role of the family. Everyone turned to Geof. When he was nineteen, due to a need to find his own identity, he moved to California.

While there, Geof enlisted himself in the US Army. He refused to settle for general infantry; instead, he worked his way through officer candidate school and became a second lieutenant and a part of the 101st Airborne Division. He was the leader of a reconnaissance platoon whose mission was to be dropped by helicopter into active war zones and report the intelligence. However, this did not mean they were free from fire fights. Among many medals and honors, Geof was awarded the Silver Star, the medal just below the Congressional Medal of Honor, for heroism in battle. One day on assignment, his battalion encountered enemy fire. While many of his men were pinned down, and some wounded, Geof crawled toward oncoming fire and enemy encampments, throwing hand grenades to end the ambush before dragging his men to safety.

This was one of the first times he was formally recognized as a leader, but it certainly would not be the last. Upon returning to civilian life, Geof took over his father's chain of drugstores, Scanlon's Drugs, for thirty years until closing the family business in 1992. In 1994, Geof started Scanlon & Associates, which became a successful insurance and investments brokerage and the parent company for the Southwest Ohio & Northern Kentucky region of BNI and the Referral Institute. My dad's social and civic contributions are too many to mention. Most of his spare time was spent volunteering at local charities. Put simply, no more room is left on the wall in his office for plaques appreciating his years of service for the impoverished, the drug-addicted, and orphanages. As a child, I learned more about his character than I ever realized when we had a young man, with no home of his own, come to live with us. I still remember Leo to this day.

Dad and I have worked together for more than twenty years. I cannot express how thankful I am to have spent that time with the best partner anyone can ask for, and the person I love more than anyone. I never felt like I worked *for* him, but *with* him. And he never gave me anything but attention, feedback, and opportunity. He made me earn it all, and that is the best thing he did for me. Our personalities complement each other so well, and our work ethics are so similar, that we experienced growth in all of our companies, year after year. What I loved the most is having lunch with him at Skyline Chili, just down the street from our office. What we have accomplished will wash away with time, but never will we lose the time we shared. There are no words for how much I cherish those times; there are only feelings—feelings of love and respect. This book is for you, Dad. Thanks for always believing in me.

Introduction

The Three Rs of Networking

Imagine waking up in a world where you spend your work week meeting face-to-face with highly qualified potential clients, returning calls and e-mail messages regarding quality referrals from current customers and other business associates, and having a trusted group of other like-minded professionals who are eager to help you succeed. No more cold calls, no more expensive advertising campaigns, and no wasting time chasing leads that go nowhere. Sounds like a wonderful fantasy world, right? But what if this "alternate reality" really does exist?

Now imagine a circle. This circle represents all of your relationships, both personal and professional. Once the circle is formed, it has no end. If you do the right things in a relationship, the circle will continue. It goes around and around, over and over, and with every rotation, the relationship improves and becomes stronger. The success of these circles, the relationships in your life, depends on one very important detail: there is no break in the circle. If there is a disconnect anywhere in the circle, like the interruption of an electrical current through a circuit, that break will stop the flow of energy. In business and personal relationships, these disconnects happen to people every day, all around the world. Why? It's simple: they have not formed the right circles. They haven't done all of the right things consistently once the circle is formed. Once the disconnect occurs, most give up on that particular relationship. But what if there were a way to keep these relationships going full circle, indefinitely? What if there were a way to ensure that *relationships* foster *referrals*, which then produce *results*? We call this the three Rs of networking: relationships, referrals, results.

Similar to the three Rs of education (reading, [w]riting, and [a]rithmetic), the three Rs of networking must happen collectively to avoid what we call the "Networking Disconnect." Just as many students resist the three Rs of education, many businesspeople resist the three Rs of networking. Why? Simply put, because it's work. It takes work to develop relationships, it takes work to give referrals, and it takes work to ensure results keep coming. When the process doesn't flow smoothly—and it often doesn't—is when people give up. They disconnect. Thomas Edison said, "Opportunity is missed by most people because it's dressed in overalls and looks like work." He also stated, "Many of life's failures are people who didn't know how close they were to success when they gave up." As you enter into this process, stay with it. Don't give up. The benefits are far too great. And remember the most important thing as you set out on this journey: it's all about the relationships.

PART 1

Focus In Before Stepping Out

The majority of business networkers are good at filling their calendars, attending functions, joining organizations, setting appointments with those they meet, spending time with a variety of people, and then drawing quick conclusions about whether or not the person they've met is worthy of their time. This is necessary, and vital, to their success. It's also absolutely self-serving. Don't get us wrong—networking without eventual sales is, by design, flawed. A pivotal notion must land with you, right here, right now, if you want any long-term success.

Ready? Here it is. Don't even think about leaving your home or office to network if you are not the most compelling and inspirational version of you possible. In other words, focus in before stepping out. Take a hard look in the mirror, and you might find that your overall identity is not yet referral-worthy. You might find that you're not even certain what sets you apart, why someone might mention you after meeting you, and why the world can or cannot live without you. Imagine investing hours, weeks, months, and years in your network and not really even knowing why you are in the very business you have chosen, who you are truly serving, and why.

CHAPTER 1

The Networking Disconnect

Ivan

I was at a big networking event. More than nine hundred people were in the audience, and I asked everyone there: "How many of you came here hoping to do some business—maybe make a sale?" Almost everyone in the audience raised their hands. I then asked, "How many of you are here hoping to buy something?" *No one raised their hand—not one single person! This is what I call the "Networking Disconnect."* Most people show up to networking events wanting to sell something, but no one is there hoping to buy something! This disconnect is why so many people hate networking. Over and over again, I read articles from well-meaning "experts" who say horrible things about networking. The problem is, they are generally experiencing "direct selling" done under the guise of networking. That's where the Networking Disconnect comes in, and that's almost always behind the reason some people don't like networking.

If you're going to networking events hoping to sell something, you're dreaming. OK, I recognize that it can happen—but it generally happens as often as a solar eclipse. It's possible that anyone can stumble over an immediate sale at a networking event, but then, even a blind squirrel can find a nut occasionally! Don't confuse direct selling with networking. Effective networking is about *developing relationships*, not using the event as a "face-to-face cold-calling" opportunity.

I recently read an article published on a major online business platform titled "Stop Networking." It went on to explain how the process of networking is so "mercenary." The problem is that every example the author gave about how networking doesn't work was an example of *really bad* networking! Their conclusion was to *stop* networking. Instead of networking, the author said you should do these five things:

1. Focus on relationships, not transactions.
2. Don't ask for something before you give something.
3. Don't make the process about you.
4. Strive for quality, not quantity, in your relationships.
5. Volunteer for leadership roles in organizations you belong to.

Hello! Does anyone notice that the emperor has no clothes? I would argue that *all* five of these strategies are about networking—the right way. In this article, bad networking tactics were presented as the reasons people should stop doing it. Networking can certainly be done badly—but networking itself isn't bad.

The key at networking events is to make solid connections with individuals so they will remember who you are when you do follow up with them. You want them to be excited to meet with you for coffee or lunch. If you go to networking events just trying to sell, those people won't want to meet with you later because they know you're going to pitch them. If you want people to be eager to meet with you after networking events, the key is to *find ways to help them.* Think back to the nine hundred people in my audience. Think about all the circles that had the possibility of forming, and connecting, and how many of them most likely didn't. If everyone in that room focused on learning who they could help, as opposed to sell, imagine the relationships that might have been. Good networking is all about building relationships.

CHAPTER 2

It's Not about Sales; It's about Relationships

Brennan

I n the spring of 1998, at the age of nineteen, I became licensed to sell life, health, and disability insurance. My father owned and operated an employee benefits brokerage and gave me my first sales job in the family business. (Yes, insurance sales. How exciting, right?) I started my sales career with a desk, a phone, and a long list of businesses to call. After hundreds of phone calls and weeks of hearing "No" to my well-crafted cold-call question, "Would you like to buy health insurance?" I found myself organizing my desk drawer, filing papers, refilling my stapler—anything to avoid that dreaded phone. When I found myself alone in the office, I would pace back and forth, wearing down a path in the carpet, feeling anxious and hopeless. I wanted to make my father proud, but I felt like I was failing. Maybe selling insurance wasn't the career for me.

Finally, as I was about to throw in the towel, I scored my first sale. Words cannot express the joy and relief I felt inside. Did I become so proficient with my cold-calling technique that something finally clicked for my potential customer? Nope. My first insurance client was actually my first *referral*. Another salesperson I had met highly recommended me to the client. I've not made a cold call since. Instead, I've received thousands of referrals and have given thousands of referrals in return. I grew my insurance business 100 percent per year for my first three years, *exclusively* by referrals.

What puts you and your business ahead of the pack? What keeps people talking about you? Attention spans are shorter than ever. According to several recent studies, you have only about *nine seconds* to capture people's attention in the busiest, most overmarketed, and overcommunicated-to society in the history of mankind. Is it possible to accomplish this in a cold call? Not likely. Fortunately, there's a proven way to break through the distractions and stand out from the masses—to be referred by someone who knows, likes, and trusts you. The best strategy to achieve long-term, sustainable business growth is to learn how to cultivate relationships that result in a predictable, steady stream of high-quality referrals. My passionate desire is to show you how to leave cold calling behind forever by developing the *richest relationships of your life*.

CHAPTER 3

Who Are You? What Do You Stand For? And Why Should I Care?

Brennan

"The universe likes speed. Don't delay, don't second-guess, don't doubt. When the opportunity is there, when the impulse is there, when the intuitive nudge from within is there…*act*. That's your job, and that's all you have to do."
—DR. JOE VITALE, AMERICAN ENTREPRENEUR AND AUTHOR

For as long as I can remember, I've had a passion for public speaking. When I'm in front of an audience, I'm in "the zone." I first discovered this at age nineteen, while giving a talk in front of high school students at a Christian Awakening retreat. I felt so alive and so perfectly in my place. At the age of twenty-two, I approached a training company about being a presenter and even took a ride along with a professional speaker to a meeting of the Columbus, Ohio, chapter of the National Speakers Association.

I had a deep-rooted desire to speak back then; however, I didn't know what subject to speak about. I knew in my heart this is what I was supposed to be doing for a living. I had been gifted with the ability to speak, but on what topic, with what passion? Over the next ten years, I presented at more than 1,400 BNI (Business Network International) meetings to groups of as few as ten people to groups as large as 350. During this time, I refined my craft even further. However, I knew there was another level for me.

It was an early weekday morning in April 2008 as I walked into a Chamber of Commerce building. I was embarking on yet another Visitors' Day meeting for BNI, not foreign territory to me. During my presentation that day, I noticed someone I will never forget. This refined older gentleman was wearing a blazer and glasses and had distinctive red hair. He sat in the back of my audience, listening intently. His eyes followed my every move, as though he could not listen closely enough. At the conclusion of the meeting, this gentleman came up to me and said the words I will always remember: "I rather enjoyed your presentation; I belong to a jewelers' association that brings in speakers. I think they would benefit from your message."

It was like the clouds parted, and my golden opportunity was presented to me. I just had to reach out and take it. I will be forever grateful to that man because the subsequent speaking engagement for his jewelers' association became the starting point of my life's work.

I now speak all over the country for a vast array of business organizations and companies. What started as a dream has now become my reality. The realization for me along the way is that I did not have to have all the answers at the beginning of my speaking career. The truth of the matter is, we never do. It's crucial to remember two things on our journey:

1. First, we must understand that we don't have to have all the answers, but we do have to stay in the game—or in my case, get in the game.
2. Second, whatever it is that keeps calling to you, whatever itch you need to scratch, listen, and scratch it until it hurts.

You see, that thing that keeps calling your name is not something you ought to do but rather something you *have* to do.

> "Everyone has talent. What's rare is the courage to follow it to the dark places where it leads."
>
> —Erica Jong, American author

So who are you, what do you stand for, and why will anyone care? Get ready to answer that question. It will have a profound impact on your career and your life.

CHAPTER 4

The Number One Question to Ask

Yourself (Hint: It's about Your Passion)

Ivan

For sixteen years, I taught classes at a state university. The college kids would come up to me and ask, "Dr. Misner, in your opinion, what are the upcoming business opportunities? What field should I go into?" Because I taught management theory, strategic planning, and social capital in the business school, my students thought I'd have insight into the hot new trends in the market.

I'd ask them a very important question in return: "What are you passionate about?"

The students would look at me with confused expressions and say, "Um, no, my question is 'What's the upcoming thing?'"

I'd reply, "I hear your question, but what are you passionate about?" One kid said to me, exasperated, "Dr. Misner, you're not listening to me!"

I countered, "No, you're not listening to *me*. I'm asking you what you're passionate about because when you tell me what you're passionate about, then I can think about what's upcoming that may have relevance to your passion."

Sadly, too many college students pick a field of study based on job openings and salary potential, only to find out later that they have no passion for it. Before wasting years of schooling and racking up tens of thousands of dollars in student loan debt, these students need to be asking themselves the right question: "What's my passion?" If they don't, they will fail miserably. It's not an abstract question, and it has to be answered personally.

I almost made this same mistake myself. I had been accepted to law school, but I didn't honestly have a passion for it. I'm a very linear thinker in many ways. I weighed the pros and cons of law school, and on paper, it seemed like the logical choice. To this day, I can't give you a good reason why I didn't go to law school. I think I understood back then, even as a young man, that I had to follow my passion. I realized that for whatever reason, at that time, law wasn't my passion. I can't tell you why it was not my passion, but I can tell you it was not my passion. I went in a different direction, following my passion, and as I look back today, I'm so happy I did.

That's why the number-one question to ask yourself is "What's my passion?" Once you've answered that question, then look for opportunities that capitalize on your skills and your passion. Now, picture a candle. The flame is dancing and bright, while the wax is thick and slowly dripping down the side. I learned long ago that I'm either working in my wax or working in my flame. When I'm working in my flame, I'm excited and energetic. I'm doing what I love, and the passion for it clearly shows. The work really doesn't seem like work because I'm doing what I love to do. These are the things that make me want to spring out of bed in the morning and seize the day. I'm on fire and everyone around me can see that I'm in my element.

On the other hand, when I'm working in my wax, I'm doing things that sap my energy. They might be tasks I'm not good at or don't enjoy doing. They may be things that aren't my skill set but still need to be checked off my list. Whatever they are, I dread doing them. They drain my energy, and I find myself procrastinating and becoming frustrated at work.

The solution to working in your wax is to remember that your wax is someone else's flame. There is another person out there who loves to do the things you hate doing. Delegate the tasks you don't like or aren't good at to your employees or outside contractors. The more time you spend in your flame, the more successful you will be. Follow your passion. Flame work is infectious.

CHAPTER 5

Finding Your Why

Stop. What are you doing in business right now and why? Imagine if you asked yourself this question before doing anything. Sure, in cases such as brushing your teeth, bathing, and eating, you don't need to explore these decisions. But what about your business activities? There is a thin line between a groove and a rut. Major changes are often unnecessary, and sometimes small ones can regain our rhythm. You may find that you hit your groove again when you redetermine your "why," also known as your ECC (Emotionally Charged Connection.)

Whether you're a CPA or a mechanic, with all due respect, we don't care. We really don't. What we care about is why you put your feet on the floor this morning and decided to stand up and go to work. There can be so many reasons, and only you know what they are. But does the rest of the world? Would you step over a winning lottery ticket if you knew it was more than a piece of paper? Would I step past you if I knew not only what you do but why you do it? People don't care much about what we do for a living, or how we operate, until they know what drives us. Most of the people we meet talk to us only about what they do, but they never explain *why*.

Let's explore the five reasons your *why* should come first.

1. **Believability**—Skepticism is at an all-time high. Think about all the different channels of communication now available to us to broadcast our message, not to mention the vast number of people and businesses vying for attention. Among TV, social media, and radio, it's enough to make anyone's head spin. It's only natural to defend ourselves from the onslaught. Automatically, people are not to be believed—that is, until they give us a compelling reason to do so.

2. **Likeability**—"Sell *yourself*, not your stuff," Virginia Musquiz said recently at a Referral Institute conference in Petaluma, California. Webster defines a "commodity" as a "mass-produced unspecialized product." Ouch! Do other people sell what you sell? If the answer is yes, you'd better get some likeability. Products and price being relatively equal, people will always choose to buy from someone they genuinely like.

3. **Authenticity**—When and how have you failed? It's true that no one wants to look bad. However, if you look perfect, that is even worse. Weave stories about your failures and imperfections into your conversations with others. If you can show some humility early on, you will shorten the trust timeline. It's OK to share with people that you make mistakes, especially if you then tell how you've fixed them.

4. **Connectivity**—What do we have in common? In a recent training session, we learned that the other people in the class enjoyed photography, cycling, cooking, nature, and running. Bonding and rapport comes when you share the same hobbies with someone else or when you are interested in learning more.

5. **Referability**—Recently an electrician told us the dramatic story about his career choice. He said, "When I was a eleven years old, my family rushed out of our home in the middle of the night due to an electrical fire in the basement. While everyone made it out all right, we lost everything—the house and all of our earthly possessions. I knew then that I never wanted this to happen to anyone else, so that's why I became an electrician." If your story is not this

dramatic, that's OK. But we still want to know the reason why you do what you do.

It makes no difference how you communicate your message, whether it's TV, radio, print advertising, billboards, Facebook, LinkedIn, Twitter, keynote presentations, or face-to-face meetings. Until we know *why*, it doesn't matter *what* you do.

CHAPTER 6

Brennan's Why

If you would have asked me ten years ago what I do for a living, you would have heard some variation of, "I'm an executive director for BNI (Business Network International)." Or "I'm an aspiring professional speaker." After years of lukewarm responses and blank, uninterested stares, I've changed the way I answer that question. I'm no longer lost in a sea of faces at networking events because my answer usually intrigues people, and they want to know more about me. Now, when asked what I do, I say, "I help people create referrals for life by helping them to create the richest relationships of their lives." So, what does it mean?

I was born on January 31, 1978, in Cincinnati, Ohio, to Ann and Geof Scanlon. We were a modest Midwestern family. I had an older sister named Kelly and an older brother named Brady. Everything was normal—that is, until, when I was five years old, my parents divorced. While it was tough on the family, it was also good for the family because my parents were not meant to stay together. In addition, it allowed me to have two great stepparents who doubled the amount of parental love and attention in my young life. Another side benefit was something any kid in the world would want: two Christmases!

However, the divorce did come with its challenges. My Mom was an emergency room nurse and was gone much of the time. She was working hard to make ends meet and raise three children. My Dad was, and still is, the hardest-working businessman I've ever known. One of the biggest challenges was the custody arrangement. I was with my Mom during the week and with my Dad on the weekends. With my Mom's schedule of being on call at the hospital, I often had less supervision during the week than a mischievous boy like myself required. I typically didn't get my discipline and structure until the weekends, when I went to my Dad's house. I would have continued to get away with it if not for one person: my older brother, Brady. At a time when I did just about whatever I wanted, he was the one who pushed me…literally, down the stairs, over the curb, and into the walls. He roughed me up, as most older brothers do, but only because he saw how soft and undisciplined I was becoming, and he wanted to toughen me up.

I remember asking myself, "Why is he so tough on me?" It wasn't until later that I realized it wasn't just because he was standing in for Dad during the week. But somehow I think he knew that he might not always be there and he had to make me better while he could. Brady and I became great friends as we grew older. I watched him get his degree in landscape architecture from Cincinnati State and develop a highly successful business, "The Four Leaf Landscaping Company," named in honor our family's Irish heritage. He had hundreds of clients and installed gorgeous landscapes for homes and companies. Then one day in October 2004, Brady called me, my Sister, and my Dad to the office. Curious to know what was up, we met him there. Brady told us that he had been diagnosed with metastatic melanoma, stage four skin cancer. What he said next I will never forget as long as I live. Brady stated, "I was hesitant to tell you guys because I was nervous about how you would take the news." What type of person contracts terminal cancer and then worries about how others will take it?

Even though it was stage four cancer, and the odds of survival were slim, Brady stayed positive. He decided to undergo chemotherapy and surgeries to remove the cancer, and he changed his diet dramatically. I remember sitting with my Dad and Brady in the hospital room in January 2005, around the time of Brady's thirty-second birthday, as he flipped through maps of the state of Kentucky from his hospital bed. As he turned the page, Brady looked at us and said, "This is the route we are going to ride this spring, guys. We'll take the motorcycles right through the Red River Gorge." We set the date then, the third weekend in May. My Father, Brady, and I would ride that weekend together to celebrate his beating this disease. That ride with Brady never happened. Brady battled the cancer for six short months, but in March 2005, he was gone.

There wasn't enough room to accommodate everyone at one funeral. It took two. Both services were standing room only, with lines of people out the door and around the block. After the dust had settled and everyone said their good-byes, I looked at my calendar and saw that date in May when we were to take that motorcycle ride together. Stunned, and numb, I just stared at it. I could not bring myself to delete it. So, after much discussion with my sister, Kelly, Mom, Dad, and the rest of our family, we decided to create the First Annual Brady Scanlon Motorcycle Ride to Remember. This was on the very weekend my dad and I were to ride with Brady.

Do you know what the best part is? We don't ride *for* him; we ride *with* him every year. And after more than a decade, hundreds of people still show up for the event. Brady's friends and past clients continue to donate thousands of dollars in his memory to help prevent others from losing their loved ones to the same disease. How is it possible that people will still support you all those years after your passing? It's simply because, while you are here on earth, you developed the absolute richest relationships of your life. Now you understand why I help people create referrals for life™ by helping them create the richest relationships of their lives. My Brother is why I do what I do. Why do you do what you do? Believe me when I tell you, it's the most important thing in your business and in your life.

CHAPTER 7

Ivan's Why

There has probably been someone in your life—a coach, grandparent, teacher, aunt, or spiritual mentor—who's made a difference for you. It may have been when you were young (it generally is) or it may have been recently. It may have been a positive experience, or it may have been very negative. Either way, it is your "why" for what you are passionate about.

I've certainly had people who have made a significant difference in my life. One of those people was my freshman high school teacher, Mr. Romero, at Gladstone High School in southern California. Mr. Romero taught history, and that class was the one that selected the student council representative for the freshmen. I had run for student council numerous times in junior high school and was soundly defeated each time. The elections weren't even remotely close. In fact, I came in dead last every time. Each election was a humiliating experience that left an indelible impression on me. So, by the time high school rolled around, I had no intention of running for student council again. *Ever!*

The first week of freshman history class, our teacher, Mr. Romero, asked all the students, "Because we pick the freshman student council representative from this year's history class, are there any volunteers for the position? Who would like to do it?" Nobody volunteered. Finally one of the prettiest, most popular girls in the class said, "Oh, Mr. Romero, you know, I would do it, but I'm just so busy! I don't have the time to do something like that."

Mr. Romero replied, "That's OK, you don't have to do it. But if no one's interested in volunteering, as the teacher, I get to pick. Are you OK with that?"

The students came back with cheers: "Yeah, yeah, yeah—you go ahead and pick!" So the teacher looked around the class, paused his gaze at me, and, looking me straight in the eyes, he said, "Ivan, I'll bet you would love to do this, wouldn't you?"

I replied, "Well, um, well, yeah, I kind of would, Mr. Romero." My momentary elation was immediately squashed when the entire class, almost in unison, moaned, "Oh, no. Not Ivan!" Even the too-busy popular girl stood up and said, "No, no, Mr. Romero. You know what—I'm actually not that busy. If you're going to pick Ivan, I can do it after all!" Of course, while she was saying all this, I was thinking, *Hello. You all see me sitting here, right?* But I couldn't actually open my mouth to speak. I just sat there, quiet and embarrassed, holding my breath. Have you ever had a moment like this? When you felt so small you just wanted to slip underneath the carpet? That was how I felt in that moment.

It's important to put this experience in context. Today, I'm an author, speaker, and fairly successful businessman with franchises on every populated continent of the world. But remember, this was happening to me as a young thirteen-year-old boy. I lacked confidence, I felt like I didn't fit in at all, and I couldn't get a chance to prove myself at something I really wanted to do. Just imagine, for a moment, how humiliating this was for me. I didn't have the advantage of peeking into the future to know where I would end up. I have to tell you, it was a raw, exposed moment.

Somehow, Mr. Romero understood that, and he gave the ever-popular girl a withering look and said, "No, you had your chance to volunteer, and you didn't take it. So I'm empowered to pick a representative, and I pick Ivan.

He's the student representative! Now, open your books and turn to chapter two."

Despite the grumbles rolling through the classroom, Mr. Romero's decision was final. I was the Student Council Representative. My teacher believed that I could do a good job. I took a deep breath in and knew I would work hard—really hard—to prove him right. When the year-end Student Council elections came around for the following year, I decided to do something I had vowed to never do again: I ran for Student Council. That same class who loudly protested my appointment voted me in for another year, by a landslide! As a matter of fact, I won every election in high school after that—Student Council, Activities Director, Student Body President—every single one. It all started with Mr. Romero seeing something in me that I had not been able to see in myself. His giving me that chance allowed me to prove myself. This infused confidence in me, and that made a huge difference in my life. I gained leadership skills and learned responsibility by being involved in those school projects that I had to take from the beginning to the end. Mr. Romero positively influenced my life by giving me the *opportunity* to succeed. He didn't do the hard work for me, but he opened the door for me. He gave me a chance to excel, to succeed, and to show what I was capable of doing.

Years later, I knew this was an important experience in my life, but I never realized how seminal it truly was to the man that I would become. It wasn't until a few years ago at a Referral Institute seminar that I came to realize that my entire life's work was in fact, a reflection of what Mr. Romero did for me as a young man. We were all studying our Emotionally Charged Connections (ECCs) to understand why we do what we do.

Every book I've written or business I've started has been an attempt to give other people an *opportunity* to succeed, to excel, and to accomplish what they want to accomplish in life. I can't "make" someone successful. Only they can do that. I can however, provide the system, the process, and the *opportunity* for them to achieve their dreams. I have been continuously reliving what Mr. Romero did for me, and I never even knew it—until I looked deeply into my "why."

Your "why" is the most important thing you can figure out right now. It is the reason you do the things you are passionate about. If you don't know that, you can never come full circle to completely fulfill your dreams.

We will be talking about the importance of your ECC later in this book. If you pick up nothing else from reading our thoughts (and we genuinely hope you pick up a great deal), you definitely want to figure out your "why" for doing what you do.

This is so important that we're going to do something that authors rarely ask a reader to do. In a moment, we want you to *put the book down* and go back in your mind to a time in your life that was a nexus point. Think about something that happened to you that dramatically changed the direction you were going or that had such a fundamental impact on who you were that it influenced the person you are today. That is your "why." It may be something big that happened in your life, or it may be something small that had a big impact. Either way, you'll know it if you go back far enough.

OK, what are you waiting for? *Step away from the book.*

CHAPTER 8

Person, Passion, and Then Profession

Brennan

Welcome back.

After taking that short break just now, you may have pondered a few reasons why you do what you do for a living. Perhaps it was when you were let go from your last job, and it became the best thing that could have happened to you. Perhaps when you stepped away, your toddler pulled on your leg and asked to be picked up. Maybe your spouse gave you a smile and a kiss. Maybe you looked at the photo of that person who made you the person you are today. Or maybe you happened to read that thank-you card your best client just sent to you. Finding the way to your why is not a quick and easy process. It takes reversing how you look at your business and at yourself. It takes the profession all but out of it. In fact, it really boils down to who you are as a person and what you are passionate about. Then and only then will others actually care about your profession. Even though your "why" may not be fully transparent yet, here is a great example of a way to begin finding it.

Imagine for a moment a successful salesperson. What does she look like? How does she earn new business? Do you envision her always on the go, hustling from prospect to prospect? Do you picture her walking across a parking lot in the rain, making some witty remark to get past the gatekeeper, and then overcoming several client objections to get a big deal done?

Why is this the stereotype that comes to mind for a successful salesperson? Perhaps it lies in the misconception that making a sale is a difficult and intense process that can only be earned through a struggle. Why is that image of salespeople taking the bull by the horns and wrestling the prospect to the ground and into submission still a relevant metaphor? I think it's because most people assume business success must be painful to achieve. However, the best sales should be easy and, well, pleasant. Yes, hard work is very much the key to success, but making the sale doesn't have to be painful or combative.

Meet one of the most successful salesmen I know: Jerry Arrasmith of Arrasmith Promotions. I've known Jerry for more than sixteen years, and we've been in the same weekly networking group for the past eight of them. Jerry helps businesses grow their bottom line through the use of branded merchandise and apparel printed with company logos. Jerry has built a tremendous business, not by standing in the rain, but rather by building a network of professional relationships that continuously send him business year after year. So how has he done this? Jerry employs what I call "The three Ps to profit: person, passion, and then profession." Let's take a look at them.

1. **Person**: First and foremost, Jerry is a warm and interesting person. I recently heard him give a keynote presentation at our weekly networking meeting, and he mentioned *nothing* about his products. Instead, Jerry connected with each of us in the meeting by sharing that his primary goal is to help us however possible. We learned that Jerry is a family man who loves golf and boating. He loves working in the family business with his father, aunt, and sister. We learned that Jerry works hard to provide a life for his wife and children, not a living for himself.

   Let's address why it's important, even in business, to know other professionals as people first. Ready? Here is the answer. It's because otherwise, *no one cares*. Wow, was that cold? No, it is reality. The fact is that we are now living in the most overcommunicated and overmarketed society in the history of mankind.

We have to be discriminating! The only way to accomplish this is listening only to those who are sincere, genuine, and real. We need this as the first step in the sequence because it allows us to let only the right people and a reasonable number of people into our lives. Otherwise, it's simply too much to process.

2. **Passion**: Next, Jerry talked about his clients, the neat things they do, and how he loves to help them succeed. He spoke about the other employees at his company and how he loves the accomplishments they work hard to achieve. Jerry shared that he's not particularly passionate about his products but about his customers' goals that his products help accomplish. In short, he has established the likeability and trust necessary for a person who has more competition than most professions.

So why is passion the next step? Not only do we need to know we are dealing with a *real* person; we also want to know that we dealing with an *authentic* person—one who has both personal and professional values, ideals, and goals. If your prospect sees you only as a potential service provider, you're automatically dead in the water! It's that simple. It's a one-dimensional perspective, and the dimension is the sales process. It's only when you become three-dimensional that you'll be seen in a new light. You'll have reached this stage when you share what you stand for, what you are compassionate about, and what interests you have in common with your prospect such as boating, golf, and family.

3. **Profession**: Finally, Jerry mentioned that he's capable of putting a company logo on anything we want, within budget and on time. This was the smallest part of his presentation, and that was refreshing. Wow! I was so excited to enjoy a ten-minute presentation in which only one minute was about the nitty-gritty details of his business. I can look at only so many pens, drink koozies, notepads, and polo shirts before my mind starts to wander! Jerry knows he has considerable competition in the marketplace. The only real differentiator he has is himself. Jerry understands the adage "Sell yourself, not your stuff."

Person, passion, and then profession. Jerry will do more business than the majority of his competitors this year. Why? Because most of his competitors are product pushers who care more about having a sales transaction than having a relationship with their clients. While they are standing outside in the rain, Jerry will be inside collecting the check.

CHAPTER 9

Are You Inspired or Just Tired?

Brennan

It's been said that there's a thin line between a groove and a rut. You work hard to get to where you are, yet you find that the daily grind of activities that has made you successful eventually bores you. So how do you keep focused on the fundamentals of success while having that excited "new day" feeling, every day? In other words, how do you live an inspired life?

The answer, to me at least, is to get emotional every day. No, I'm not recommending that you cry tears of joy (or sorrow) every morning. I am suggesting that you start your day, or end it, with that thing that puts the fire in your soul. For me, it's my brother's well-worn boots that I see every time I pull into and out of my garage.

A few weeks after Brady's funeral, my dad dropped off a pair of work boots on my desk chair at the office while I was out calling on clients. They were by no means new. It was clear that they had seen many years of hard labor. After a few days had passed, I ran into my dad and finally asked about the boots. He said, "Those were your brother's. I thought you'd like to have them." My brother was a landscape architect and worked ten-hour days. He poured his heart and soul into his work and his relationships with his clients, his family, and his friends. Some people may see old work boots, but I see commitment. I see perseverance, and I see inspiration. That is why Brady's boots are the last thing I see when I leave the house and the first thing I see when I get home.

The boots themselves? Worth nothing. What they stand for? Worth everything. The secret to living an inspired life starts with whatever inspires *you*. You can't find it; you aren't that good. Neither am I. You have to be quiet and open long enough to let it find you. A portion of the vision statement for Referral Institute Cincinnati reads, "Referral Institute Cincinnati is known for helping our clients discover, or rediscover, the reason they are in business…" Maybe you have yet to discover your true inspiration. Or maybe you need to rediscover and reignite your passion. There is a third possibility, and it's the one that frightens and saddens me the most. That is the situation in which an individual has no inspiration and doesn't even realize it. Instead, that person goes through the motions, day in, and day out. Some people will do this their entire lives. I'll bet you did not know that a book on networking would go this "deep." *The core of any referrals you'll receive lie exclusively in this area.* Tired people don't get regular referrals. Only inspired people get regular referrals.

CHAPTER 10

Refuel Your Motivation

Ivan

Some time ago, one of my blog readers asked me these excellent questions: "Ivan, what do you do when your motivation level and self-esteem are lacking? How do you regain the motivation you need to move forward with your plans and pursue your endeavors?"

First of all, let me say that I am as certain of what I'm about to tell you as anything in my life—motivation comes from *within you*, not from outside of you. No one can motivate you but yourself. I'm speaking of long-term motivation. Many years ago, in the *Harvard Business Review*, Frederick Herzberg wrote about motivation and said that others can motivate you, but only in the short term. He called that "KITA" (Kick in the... Anatomy—yes, that's really what he called it).

Long-term motivation, on the other hand, comes from within. So that begs the question "How do you inspire yourself when your motivation is low? It's vital to understand that everyone deals with this at times. I've never met anyone who was immune to it, including me. So what do I do when I feel down? Here are some of the things that have helped me.

1. **Minimize contact with negative people!** You probably can't avoid negative people completely, but shield yourself as much as you can. Some people complain as though it was an Olympic event and they

are going for the gold! Keep clear of the downers while you're trying to get your mojo back.

2. **Maximize time with people and activities that refuel your energy!** You become like the five or six people you hang out with the most. Spend time with people who make you want to *"do"* and *"be"* better. Read, listen, and watch positive things. If you are feeling down, read an uplifting book. Listen to a podcast with a positive message or some upbeat music. Watch a movie or TV show that makes you laugh until your sides hurt! Surround yourself with things and people who make you feel happy. Let that joy into your life as much as possible.

3. **Prioritize the things you want to do and must do.** Make a list. I live by lists. The more I can get a handle on the things I need and want to do, the easier it is to tackle them. Eat the elephant one bite at a time. Take that list you've created, and tackle a few items on that list *every day*. If you consistently do this, you'll be amazed at how much you get accomplished. The more you achieve, the better you will feel. They feed each other.

Networking and growing your business through referral marketing requires work! There will be times when you feel your motivation slipping. When you do, review the above list of ideas for staying fired up and inspired. The point is to be aware of your motivation level and make a conscious effort to bring it back up when it starts to drop.

CHAPTER 11

Rediscovering Your Business:

Find Your Starting Point

I f you want others to send you high-quality referrals, then you must teach them how to do this. They must know exactly what you do: the product or service you provide or make, how and under what conditions you provide it, how well you do it, and in what ways you are better than your competitors. You have to communicate this information to your referral sources effectively. To do that, you must first know the same things.

This seems like a no-brainer. Don't we all know what we do for a living? Of course we do. But can you communicate it to your potential sources clearly and simply? You may find that you're not as clear on the facts as you thought. If you can't tell your potential sources exactly what you do or what you sell, how can they send you good referrals?

1. Reexamine Who You Are

Take a few minutes to get a clear picture of where your business stands today. You may think you know why you're in business, but perhaps it's been years since you have given it serious thought. Now is a good time to reexamine why you're doing what you're doing. Ask yourself these questions, and write down your answers.

1. Why are you in business, other than to make a living? Why do you do what you do? How does it serve others?
2. What do you sell? Most importantly, what are the benefits of your products or services?
3. Who are your customers? What are your target markets? Be very specific; look at segments of your business to determine your target niche(s).
4. What are your core competencies? What do you do best? What are your strengths?
5. How well do you compete? How do you stand out from your competition?

Answering these questions will help you tell others what your business is all about. This will make you more effective at implementing a comprehensive and systematic referral system.

2. Clearly Communicate Who You Are

Once you've written down your answers, think about how you can communicate this information effectively to your referral sources. How you communicate with others is very powerful. In *From Selling to Serving*, Lou Cassara states, "Your Personal Value Statement (PVS) provides the opportunity for your clients, staff, and family to market you effectively. You can build a distribution channel of people who can effectively communicate your value."

We are so accustomed to the ubiquitous question "What do you do?" that we hardly give any thought about how we answer that question. It's not enough to simply tell your contacts what label you wear, such as, "I own and operate a sporting goods store." Telling people our job title doesn't get them excited about sending business our way. To deepen the relationship, you must be able to talk about what you do in a way that, as Cassara says, "communicates the magic of your vision expressed through your words."

Too many business professionals and companies try to be all things to all people. Focus on the few things you do really well. Document those things and your vision in a way that you can communicate to others. By under-standing clearly what you do, you will be better able to communicate this to your referral sources. When you do this effectively, you are teaching your referral sources how they can refer you.

Here's a quick test to check and see how effectively you're educating your referral sources. Ask them what they say about you and your business to other people, and listen intently. Are they using the right words, phrases, and ideas to describe your products and services? If not, you have more work to do!

Let look at an example of someone who found her words and is now able to communicate her vision in an intriguing way.

CHAPTER 12

The Financial Lifeguard Finds

Her Starting Point

When introducing herself to others at networking events, Christine made the common mistake we discussed in the previous chapter. She would tell people her job title: "Hi, I'm Christine Luken. I'm a financial coach." It is the truth, but it doesn't capture your attention and make you curious to know more about what she does. We'll examine Christine's story and see how she was able to harness the passion she has for helping others with their personal finances by only changing *one word* in her introduction.

Let's rewind to a time when Christine was fresh out of high school. Thinking she was deeply in love, she started dating a new boyfriend named "Jeff." Over the course of the next seven years, Christine and Jeff's relationship changed from that of boyfriend and girlfriend to one where she referred to him as her "child." This is because, among other things, she was always cleaning up his financial messes. Jeff spent his money on drugs, was in and out of jail, and had seventeen different jobs over the course of their relationship. He would spend his money, and often her money, without Christine's knowledge. She earned the only steady income in the relationship, and out of love, or youthful ignorance, she supported him.

Unfortunately, this led to bailing him out of jail on two separate occasions, owing three different payday-lending companies money, and being months behind on their car payments. Christine no longer had the ability to write checks for her groceries because she bounced so many that all the area grocery chains blacklisted her. She was no stranger to having collections companies calling day and night, all resulting in her ruined credit. This became an unfortunate reality for Christine. Despite all this, Christine and Jeff were engaged to be married. She had a wedding dress hanging in the closet, and Jeff bought her a diamond engagement ring—which required his mother to be a cosigner.

Here's a twist you'd never see coming: Christine, with a bachelor's degree in accounting, was the accounting manager for her father's multimillion-dollar business. After years of persistence, Christine's dad finally convinced her to cut Jeff loose. And she did, thankfully *before* the wedding. Her parting words to her fiancé, while sitting on a park bench by the lake in their apartment community were, "Jeff, I feel like I am swimming across a lake and you are holding onto my leg. If I don't kick you off I am going to drown. It's over." The reason she stayed with him so long was because she saw potential in him and tried to "save" him.

Christine's dad and stepmom threw her a lifeline—a way out—and she was able to stay with them for a few months to get back on her feet. Her dad helped her formulate a budget and a plan to pay off her debts, and he schooled her on the principles of sound money management. He was Christine's helping hand when she felt like she was "going under" financially. After getting herself straightened out, Christine decided she wanted to use her experience to help others in the same situation.

Today, Christine helps people who feel like they are drowning financially get to a safe place and catch their breath, and then she teaches them how to "swim." She sits down with families and helps them devise a plan to get out of debt, build up their savings, and manage their monthly cash flow. Here are a few of her tips:

- It's OK to have room for fun in your budget; just make sure it's a reasonable amount of fun. Taking the kids to McDonald's three times a month is probably OK, but three times a week may be more than a family can afford. Let the kids pick which three times they want to go.

- Save money at the grocery store by making a list—and leaving the kids at home.
- Don't pay your children an allowance, pay them commissions. If they work, they get paid; if they don't work, they don't get paid!
- It's important for engaged couples to get "financially naked" together before tying the knot.

Now, when Christine is at a networking event, she introduces herself this way: "Hi, I'm Christine Luken, the *financial lifeguard*." Suddenly, eyebrows go up. People want to know more. By changing her title from financial coach to financial lifeguard, she has created a brand for herself that distinguishes her from the other financial professionals in the room. People understand how scary drowning feels, and now they have the image that Christine is going to jump in and pull them to safety when it feels like they're tossed about by a stormy financial situation. Should all financial coaches start referring to themselves as "financial lifeguards"? Probably not. It works for Christine because it connects on several levels with her personal experience.

Why are you doing what you're doing? What is *your* story? Is there a way you can connect elements of your story into the way you talk about yourself and your business? When you combine your passion with inspirational language, it moves people to both purchase from you and refer you to others.

CHAPTER 13

Inspirational Language, Delivered

with Passion, Moves People

Brennan

The sun is beginning to rise over the foggy mountain range. It's calm and quiet. The temperature is a cool 44 degrees. You strap on your helmet and pull down your visor. With jacket zipped and gloves tight, you look left and right to see your friends ready to ride. You hit the ignition and feel the rumble beneath you. You slowly pull away from the cabin and take the winding road that leads to the Red River Gorge. As you lean into the next curve, your favorite song fills your earphones. The wind is brisk as you speed up to forty-five miles per hour. The hikers and campers are still asleep in their tents as you lean into the road that rolls left and then right. The taillights ahead are beaming as they shine through the slowly lifting fog. The sun now shines brightly over the ridges and rock faces.

All that's ahead of you is blue sky and a two-lane road. It is at this moment that you realize how thankful you are and how fortunate you are to be free. It is at this moment you think of all the people out there who haven't experienced this feeling yet. It is at this moment that you hope and pray that whatever road will lead them there, they soon find it, just as you, my friend, have found yours.

Are you there with me? What experience am I describing? Most importantly, if I were selling you something, what would it be? In giving this presentation as a keynote, I often hear people in the audience respond with, "Freedom, peace, independence, a feeling!" They are all correct, but what product am I selling? To this, I hear, "A car, a motorcycle!" Ah-ha. Correct. This is an actual description of a motorcycle ride I took with friends. In an attempt to sell you a motorcycle, I would likely say, "It's a Yamaha Roadstar Warrior, 1700CC 102 cubic inch, air-cooled V-twin engine. It has five speeds, belt driven, with forty-one-millimeter Kayaba inverted forks. It has single shock suspension with dual 298 millimeter disk brakes." Are you still awake? You probably don't care about those details, do you? What do you really want? You want to take that hairpin turn with confidence and power, and all you really want is for the bike to perform so that you can have the *feeling* I described earlier! However, when we describe or market our products or services, no one really cares about our stuff; they only care about their outcomes. Features tell, but benefits sell. It's actually inspirational language, delivered with passion, that moves people.

Let's break that down. Does the language, or words, you choose to describe your business matter? Yes! Is it vitally important that you deliver those words with passion? Yes! And if you do that, does it move people? Yes! It moves them two ways. First, it moves them emotionally. Then it moves them financially. People decide to buy based on emotion, and *then* they back it up with logic.

All too often, we describe our businesses from the features perspective. Why do we do this? It's because the features are the easiest thing to describe. Let's look at a vacuum cleaner as an example.

CHAPTER 14

Features Tell but Benefits Sell

The year was 1957. Imagine for a moment a humble family living in the Midwestern United States: a husband, wife, and four kids under the age of twelve. Struggling to make ends meet, the father, desperate to earn a better income and a better life for his family, started selling vacuum cleaners door to door. After a slow start, including visiting a lot of houses, and receiving plenty of rejection, he went on to become one of the best in the vacuum business and even had salesmen working underneath him. The father was on the road much of the time, leaving his wife home alone to tend to their four children. His career had its ups and its downs. Even in those hard times, when asked how things were going in the vacuum business, his common and upbeat response was, "It sucks, but it's always picking up." At times, he was making a small fortune; at times, he was nearly broke. After sixteen years of hard work, building a business from scratch, he saved enough to invest in real estate. In 1975, he purchased a recently closed vacuum store and reopened the doors, calling it "All Vacuum Center." This man's name was Jim Cain.

His youngest son, Steve, the family handyman, went to work for him fresh out of high school that same year. Steve made an agreement with his father: "Dad, you're the salesman; I'm the handyman. You sell 'em, and I'll fix 'em." Steve confided in his Dad, saying, "I like this job because I have no idea how much money I will have made until the end of the year." Just like his father, another entrepreneur was born. With that comment and in that opportunity, Steve Cain, the second generation of All Vacuum Center, envisioned the opportunity to be as successful as he wanted to be and to one day take over the family business.

Unfortunately, that day came much sooner than he expected when his dad passed away only a few years later, at the age of fifty-nine. That left Steve, still in his twenties, to take over the family business and to become the primary source of income for his widowed mother.

As a legacy to his father, Steve kept All Vacuum Center at its original location for many years before opening two new locations. Since the passing of his father, Jim, Steve has sold thousands of vacuum cleaners and air purifiers. The company prides itself in selling only the "best in breed" of vacuum cleaners. Steve loves to joke with his clients by saying, "Thank goodness for Walmart, Target, and Sears for selling the cheapest vacuums known to man."

Steve's heartwarming story certainly endears people to him and gives them a reason to do business with All Vacuum Center over the big-box stores, but it's not enough. Steve still has to educate people about his superior products. Earlier, we learned that inspirational language, delivered with passion, moves people. It's also important to understand that "Features tell, but benefits sell." As an example, let's cover the features of one of Steve Cain's top-of-the-line vacuums. If you were in the market to buy, he'd tell you that this machine has the highest suction rating J. D. Power gives, with "level suction," which means the vacuum's suction will be as good in the tenth year as it does in the first. Steve could say it has a nonbreaking belt, top speed brush roll, and soft rubber wheels that swivel 360 degrees. Plus, it's equipped with a 99 percent efficient HEPA-filtered exhaust, and finally a personal guarantee.

If Steve told you all this, would you be "moved" to buy? I wouldn't, either. But what if he explained that these features lead to the best benefit of all: a doubled life expectancy of your expensive carpet because the vacuum cleaner won't leave dirt behind? Your toddler can eat animal crackers off of the floor *without* eating dirt and pet hair. Your expensive hardwood floors will remain in perfect condition. Your entire family will breathe easily in a dust-free, allergen-free home. Finally, if anything goes wrong with your vacuum, you can rely on the fifty-five-year legacy and reputation of Jim and Steve Cain, who have always done right by their customers. Sound better? Even Steve, with an amazing back story, needs to explain how his vacuums enhance the lives of his customers, not just recite a litany of product features. When all of these elements come together, customers want to buy. And they're not really buying a vacuum cleaner—they're buying a clean and healthy home.

Inspirational language packaged with a great benefits-focused message helps create binding relationships with others.

Part 1
Focus In Before Stepping Out—Recap

Takeaways

- First find your passion, and then look for opportunities that capitalize on that passion plus your skills and experience.
- At networking events, virtually everyone is looking to make a sale, though few are seeking to make a purchase. This is the Networking Disconnect.
- You should tell people *why* you do what you do first. This increases believability, likeability, authenticity, connectivity, and referability.
- Good news! Selling your product or service doesn't have to be painful or combative when you remember the Three Ps to Profit: person, passion, and then profession.
- Get emotional—inspired—every day. It's the inspired people who receive regular referrals.
- Refuel your motivation by minimizing contact with negative people, maximizing time with positive people and activities you enjoy, and prioritizing the things you need to accomplish.
- If you want people to send you high-quality referrals, it's your responsibility to teach them how to do this.
- Talk more about the *solutions* you provide more than the *products* you sell. People decide to buy based on emotion, and then back it up with logic.

Questions to Ponder

- Who are you? What do you stand for? Why will anyone care?
- What are you passionate about?
- Have you made a difference in the lives of others? Has someone like a Mr. Romero influenced positive changes in your life?
- What is that one thing that puts the fire in your soul? Are you inspired, or just tired?
- Are you spending more time working in your wax or in your flame? What "wax work" can you delegate or outsource to others?
- What steps will you take to refuel your motivation when it begins to lag?
- Why are you in business? How do you serve others?
- What do you sell? What are the benefits of your products and services?
- What are your core competencies?
- Are your words inspirational, are they delivered with passion, and do they move people?
- What does your ideal customer look like? What are your niche markets?
- How well do you compete? How do you stand out from the competition?

Don't Make a Move before Making a Plan

Then are two profound and timeless phrases that most everyone has heard over the years. The first one is to speak from your heart, not your head. The second one is to work smarter, not just harder. Just as we've presented them to you in that order, we also encourage you to see them through in that order. You learned in Part 1 how, and why, to speak from the heart. And even though you might not be sitting across from your ideal referral partner, when you do this, your message will go that much further. But what if you were sitting across from your ideal referral partner? Imagine the impact then.

What if your message landed masterfully with the exactly appropriate audience, and it happened over and over again? This would be working very smart. Part 2 of this book will challenge you to be very strategic about how you grow your business and with whom you network. Networking in the right circles is pivotal to your success. The three Rs to reconnect begins with relationships, that is for certain. From that, good referrals must result in quality business. There are generally four ways to grow your business, but we think you will find that referrals might just stand out as the best.

CHAPTER 15

Four Ways to Grow Your Business

You want sustainable growth in your business, but where do you begin? Success expert and author Brian Tracy said, "When all you have is a hammer, the whole world looks like a nail." Let's resolve right now to do more than walk around with a hammer. Let's be a little more strategic and begin by identifying the four ways to grow your business and examining the pros and cons of each.

1. Advertising

This is often the first place businesses go to drive growth, especially if they don't know where else to start. Numerous advertising options are available, including radio, TV, print, coupons and other promotions, the Internet, newsletters, billboards, bus benches, newspapers, and even posting your business card on the church bulletin board. (Please be sure to put at least five dollars in the collection plate if this is a part of your marketing campaign!)

The Pros of Advertising

- You have the potential to reach masses of people in a short time frame.
- Typically, very little work or effort is required on your part because you're paying an expert to do it for you.
- Advertising can generate a large volume of leads for your business.

- You have the ability to target prospects with very specific demographics and in different geographic areas.

The Cons of Advertising

- It can be the most expensive way to grow your business, so be prepared to write some big checks.
- If your advertising campaign isn't strategically executed, you could walk away empty-handed.
- Eighty percent of sales come after at least *five impressions* or contacts with potential customers, so your business can't dabble in advertising and expect to get results. You'll need to commit to a long-term advertising strategy.
- You may end up with a high number of low-quality leads.
- Consumers are bombarded with ads, so it can be difficult to break through the clutter and capture their attention.

According to Doug Smith, a radio advertising expert in Cincinnati, "Too many businesses look at advertising as an *expense*, when it should be viewed as an *investment*, which often leads to pulling the plug on a marketing campaign before it has time to work."

2. Public Relations

Public relations (PR) manages the message between a company or individual and the public. Good PR helps build visibility, boost credibility, and enhance the reputation of a brand or company through storytelling, and by promoting a company's products and services. This is usually accomplished through press releases, feature stories on TV news broadcasts, and/or articles in newspapers, magazines, or websites.

The Pros of PR

- It's a cost-effective approach to building positive awareness about a brand.

- PR is an efficient tool for building credibility, especially through media relations.
- The third-party endorsement and support of a quality journalist who covers a story about your company can be invaluable.
- PR can enhance and amplify other marketing efforts.

The Cons of PR

- PR is generally about brand building; it's not about immediate sales.
- It takes some time to build relationships with both journalists and the public. PR results are not instantaneous.
- Measuring the results of any marketing initiative is critical. However, it is often difficult to evaluate the success of PR campaign.

Public relations can be tricky because it's not traditional marketing. In truth, PR is the perception of your company when you are not focused on your profits. Cresta Lewis of C. Lewis Communications explains why enlisting the help of a PR professional can be worth the investment. "A good public relations person will be able to save businesses both time and money because he or she already has relationships with journalists and TV reporters and can also assist with storytelling and writing. This person will also know which media outlets will most likely be interested in running a business's story."

3. Cold Calling

Ninety-seven percent of salespeople don't like to make cold calls. That means that the remaining 3 percent who *claim* to like cold calling either are lying or are gluttons for punishment. If so many salespeople hate cold calling, why do they continue to do it? I think it's because cold calling seems to be the most direct route to conceivable new business. We've all met the person who landed the "deal of a lifetime" as a result of a cold call, and unless those stories disappear, neither will cold calling.

The Pros of Cold Calling

- It allows you to hone your skill of leaving the perfect voicemail message that will never be returned by the majority of your prospects.
- You will meet plenty of new people, mostly stoic gatekeepers of the individuals you really want to see.
- Cold calling builds character, which is supposedly good for you.
- If you make enough cold calls, someone will eventually take pity on you and buy something.

The Cons of Cold Calling

- It's a *cold* call.
- You have to make hundreds of them to see any shred of evidence that you're succeeding.
- You have to follow up on hundreds of them.
- People will lie to you and reject you most of the time.

It's been said that the only reason people make cold calls is that they have no one else to talk to, and they're under pressure to make a sale. It's our opinion that cold calls still exist for one reason: the lack of a strong referral network sending warm leads your way.

4. Networking and Referrals

One of the best opportunities for new business comes in the form of a referral. A referral is not only the most qualified form of new opportunities but also and, most importantly, it's a compliment to you and your business. Think about it: there is often nothing to gain on the part of the person giving the referral except his or her desire to recognize how great you are by allowing you to take care of family, friends, and business associates.

The Pros of Networking and Referrals (according to *Rough Notes*, a life insurance trade magazine)

- Referred clients have a 300 to 700 percent higher closing ratio than cold-call leads.
- Referred clients stay with you four times longer than nonreferred clients.
- Referred clients buy from you three to four times more in the first year than other customers do.
- Referred clients are 2.5 times more likely to refer you later to their family, friends, and business associates.
- It costs nothing to gain a referred lead.

The Cons of Networking and Referrals

- Quality referrals cannot be purchased; they must be earned with the investment of time and energy.
- Without a system or strategy, referrals will be infrequent and random.
- Profitable referral relationships take longer to develop because they're based on trust.

Now that you're familiar with the four ways to grow your business, and the pros and cons of each, you're now able to make an educated decision about what would work best for your business. It's likely that you'll use (or have used) a unique blend of all four of them. But we hope you'll put a much bigger emphasis on growing your qualified referrals instead of cold calling. Referrals are the least costly form of business growth and typically produce better long-term results.

CHAPTER 16

Successful Networkers Build

Deep Relationships

Ivan

If your network is a mile wide and an inch deep, it will never be very powerful. You need a strong and stable network that is *both* wide and deep. Like the supporting roots of a huge oak tree, some of your referral relationships need to go deeper. You create deeper relationships by learning as much as you can about other people. You want to find out details about their family, their interests, and their goals. Get to know them a little bit better.

I think the absolute master at this is definitely Harvey Mackay, a speaker and best-selling motivational author. The first time I spoke to Harvey on the phone, he must have been taking notes about everything I said. The second time I had a conversation with him, Harvey surprised me by asking, "So, how are your kids? You've got three, right? What are Ashley and Cassie doing now? And how's Trey doing—is he about ready to go to college?"

I was thinking, "Wow! How did you remember all that?" The more I spoke to Harvey, the more I became convinced that he had a system for keeping track of the important details of the people in his network.

Now when I talk to him, I know what he's doing, and I love it! I'm impressed by Harvey's system because it takes work. He has a database of the people in his network, and he does some research before calling anyone. And he's continually adding and updating the information—your pets' names, your children's names, your birthday, and the anniversary of your company startup. Harvey sets himself apart by putting in an effort to honor people by remembering what's important to them. It's hard not to be impressed by that.

That's what I mean by going deep with your relationships. Are there other ways to do this? Certainly, but I think Harvey Mackay's system is excellent. We live in this sound-bite society in which most people want to get right down to business without getting to know the other person. What I've found is when you *really* get to know somebody, amazing things happen.

Here's a good example of this. In our BNI groups, we introduced a tool called the GAINS profile—it stands for "Goals, Accomplishments, Interests, Networks, and Skills." We tested it on a small group of people to see if it would work. Each person filled it out for themselves, listing their goals, accomplishments, interests, networks, and skills—both personal and professional. Two guys in our test group didn't want to fill out their GAINS profiles. "This is just silly," they complained.

I said, "That's why we're testing this tool with you guys before we roll it out. If it doesn't work, then tell us. But you have to try it first."

So these two skeptical guys had a conversation and shared their goals, accomplishments, interests, networks, and skills with each other. During the process, they discovered that they were both coaches for their sons' soccer teams. Oh, all of a sudden, these guys were best friends! They talked about soccer and shared plays with each other. They even ended up scouting out the competition for one another's teams. And guess what happened? These guys had known each other for a year but never did business with each other. Within three months of the GAINS exercise, they were passing quality referrals to each other. The change happened because they found out they were both soccer coaches and the game connected them. That connection built trust, which turned into business.

Connecting over a nonbusiness interest endears you to the other person. Now you're not just some salesperson to them—you're a friend.

I know a businesswoman named Laura who has always wanted to travel to Greece. One of her networking connections found out in conversation about her dream to go to Greece someday. This person went out and bought Laura two simple things as a "thank you" for something she did: a calendar of beautiful places in Greece and a coffee-table book about Greece. They were fast friends after that! Because of the business associate's thoughtfulness, that connection deepened because she gave Laura tangible proof of her recognition and support of her goal. You pay a compliment to people when you show that you understand what's important to them. Make it an aim of yours to learn at least one goal or personal interest someone has *outside* of their business.

CHAPTER 17

Be Self-Aware, Selfless, and then Selfish

Let's face it, networking is about you. Yet that's the problem. Every day, millions of business seekers walk into networking events with one thing in mind: themselves. Don't feel guilty; it's totally natural. It's also counterproductive. Although you shouldn't apologize for being a product of your baser (and selfish) instincts, you need to be aware of them when networking for new business. So, are you destined to be a self-centered, one-way, "What's in it for me" sponge? No! Here is some advice on how to manage it: be self-aware, selfless, then selfish.

Be self-aware. Never walk into an event or enter into a business relationship without knowing what you want from it. Does that sound cold and impersonal? It's not. It's smart because you need a plan. Although most people think this way, not all will admit it! This is an exercise you need to complete before leaving the office.

First, you must know your target market. Does the person you're speaking to represent your target market or at least have the ability to connect you with those people? Second, you need to have a proven process to move people from prospect to paying client. Third, you must know how many of these prospects you need to reach your monthly goals. This may seem selfish, but it's really not. By doing this, you are respecting both your time and that of others. However, this may require up-front effort and patience with the process.

Be selfless. This is what our dear parents taught us while we were growing up. Now that you've determined what it will take to grow your business, it's time to motivate your potential referral sources to think of you when they hear of someone who needs your products and services. The only way this will happen is if you absolutely lose yourself in your new friend. Have you ever had a conversation with someone who hung on every word you said while making spectacular eye contact? Then every time you saw that person later, he or she did it again? Brennan has a great example of this.

> Her name is Shelley Frommeyer, and she is my financial advisor, whom I met through networking. I've met hundreds of financial advisors over the years, and I've seen all their fancy charts and graphs. But when it came time for me to choose one of them to handle my personal investments, you'll never guess what I did. Rather than analyzing the various advisors' charts on investment strategy, I sat and pondered, "Which advisor spent the most time listening to me? Who offered me support and ideas without expecting anything in return?" Ultimately, I chose the financial advisor who showed me that she cared about me as person, not just a commission. Shelley taught me a great deal; she got my business by being *selfless*.

Be selfish. You may have been getting a little anxious, but now you can relax and be a *little* selfish. Have you ever given a lot of business to someone and received *nothing* in return? Now, if it's your parent or a close personal friend, you can forgive that transgression. For all others, you've earned the right to have the favor returned. So, if you know what you want from that relationship and you've made a lot of deposits into it, examine the reasons why they're not reciprocating. Perhaps you haven't taken the time to educate them properly. Do they understand what kind of referrals you'd like, of what quality, how many, and how you'd like to be introduced? You've earned the right but have not given them the knowledge required to help you. You've not trained your referral partner, and that, my friend, is all *your fault*. Arrange a time to meet with your referral sources and arm them with the information they need to start sending business your way.

There is a rhythm and a science to the relationship process. Ask yourself the question, "Does my business rely on referrals?" If the answer is yes, then understand that referrals come from *people*. Referral marketing is unlike any other form of lead generation in that you are 100 percent reliant on other people to be successful. So why put forth the effort? The answer lies in a survey conducted by the US Chamber of Commerce in 2002. Nationwide, business owners responded that while they closed only 2 percent of cold calls, 75 to 85 percent of referrals resulted in closed business. That makes them worth pursuing, having a system to go after them, and learning how to motivate people to give them to you. Cultivating referrals takes time, patience, and a commitment to the process. Are you willing to make that investment? Are you willing to be self-aware, be selfless, and then be selfish? Allow me to share a secret: the middle is definitely the hardest part!

Now, before you head out the door to your next event, you need to ask yourself some questions so you can make the most of every networking opportunity.

CHAPTER 18

Your Networking Strategy:

Three Essential Questions to Ask

As a time-strapped businessperson, how do you figure out which networking events to attend and which you should skip? A networking strategy can help you decide which events are worth your time. Here are three easy—and essential—questions you need to answer to create a plan that will work for you.

Question #1: Who are my best prospects?

You'd be surprised at the number of business professionals who can't define their best prospects clearly. Most of them either reply, "Everyone!" or answer with some other vague description that sounds good on the surface but doesn't offer specifics. This is why business professionals so often find themselves running all over town trying to attend every networking event that comes down the pike.

Because serial networkers don't have time to follow up immediately with the people they meet, they often don't see results in the way of increased sales. So they throw their hands in the air and wail, "Networking doesn't work for me!" But as a smart, enterprising businessperson, you already know that networking works. It's just a matter of developing a strategy that connects you with the right people and allows you the time to follow up with them properly.

Some people aren't even sure what their "ideal prospects" look like. It's easy to go back and take a look at your past client list. Who are your very best customers? What industries are they in? How long have they been in business? Are your customers businesses or individuals?

Steve Cain of All Vacuum Center provides a good example of how this works. You might be thinking that his customer is anyone who needs a vacuum cleaner, right? Not really. Steve Cain would say that his ideal customer is a woman with children or pets (or both) who likely lives in a very nice neighborhood and drives a Lexus, BMW, Mercedes Benz, or Infiniti. She is most concerned with the health of her family and a quality product, not someone shopping for a bargain-basement deal. Why is it important to be this specific? Because if Steve tells you to send him anyone who needs a vacuum cleaner, does anyone come to your mind right now? Probably not. But if Steve says you should send him busy women with kids and pets who drive luxury cars or SUVs, a particular person is more likely to pop into your head.

Once you've put together a profile of the people you've worked with in the past, pick up the phone and run it by a few trusted friends and colleagues. Those who are close to you will have insights into patterns that you tend to overlook because you're busy with day-to-day operations. Once you get that nailed down, you can go on to the next question.

Question #2: Where can I meet my best prospects—or people who can introduce me to my prospects?

Networking doesn't mean just hopping into the car and attending the next Chamber of Commerce event. Yes, the chamber and other business associations are excellent means of finding and meeting new prospects, and we recommend them as a great starting point. But as your business evolves and you begin targeting specific niche markets, there are other venues that fall outside typical networking events. And that's the kind of out-of-the-box thinking we're going to discuss here.

Generally speaking, if you're trying to meet more small-business owners, you'll want to spend time at your local Chamber of Commerce, a local business association, or a referral group. Not only do these groups have exactly the type of audience you want to meet, but also with referral groups, typically a system is in place that helps you help others get more referrals for you.

If your business is geared more toward consumers, then getting involved with your kids' events—Little League, Girl Scouts, or your church's youth group—is another good way to meet the right people.

If you're that real estate agent who wants to meet first-time homebuyers and people interested in moving downtown, you'll probably find more prospects by networking at downtown events. It doesn't matter which event, as long as it's being held in the center of the city. That should bring you into contact with people who might be thinking about moving out of their apartment and into a house. Look also for networking events that young professionals are likely to attend because these are the people most likely to be living in an apartment while accumulating the disposable income to buy a downtown condo or home.

If you're looking to meet executives from large corporations in your area, we recommend service clubs, nonprofit groups, and volunteer work. Why? The directors and CEOs of large companies are less likely to be at your local chamber's after-hours event than in civic organizations like Habitat for Humanity, Kiwanis, or Rotary. We also suggest trying to get on your service club's board or leadership team. That way, you're interfacing with more of the movers and shakers of your community.

Be careful, though: if you're too direct in these clubs, too blatantly looking for business, you won't be welcomed. These groups are more civic than sales-oriented, which means you'll have to establish your credibility through community-oriented activities rather than business deals. However, once people know, like, and trust you, referrals will likely come your way over time.

Question #3: Who, exactly, do I want to meet?

Most people are not well connected in any practical sense. However, even accomplished networkers sometimes fail to realize that they're closer to a much-desired contact than they imagine. The principles behind making the right kind of connection can be summed up in the simple adage "You don't know who they know."

The idea is that the more networks you're connected to, the greater the chance that there's a short chain of contacts between you and anyone you'd care to meet. All you have to do is recognize that fact and ask a few people a specific question or two. The answers will either put you in direct contact with a prospect or lead you in the direction of the networking events you need to attend. Even if you can't name the specific people you want to meet, the better you can describe them, the greater the chance that you'll get to meet your ideal contact. The secret ingredient in this principle is specificity.

The way to meet the unknown contact is to be as detailed as possible without being too exclusive. You can do this by starting your question like this: "Who do you know who...?" Complete the sentence with specifics: "Who do you know who is a new parent?" "Who do you know who belongs to an organization that builds houses for the homeless?" By asking for a particular kind of contact, you focus the other person's attention on details that are more likely to remind him or her of a specific person than if you ask, "Do you know anyone who needs my services?"

Finally, remember that it's important to surround yourself with quality business contacts because the best way to your ideal contact very often is through someone you already know.

CHAPTER 19

Standing in the Middle of Referrals

Ivan

We are all, each and every day, standing in the middle of referrals. They are all around us; we just aren't paying enough attention to them. Part of our brain has something called a "Reticular Activating System" or RAS. Your RAS is like a filter between your conscious mind and your subconscious mind. It is capable of taking instructions from your conscious mind and passing them on to your subconscious mind. For example, maybe you've been in a busy airport with announcements coming over the loudspeaker, noise from all the hustle and bustle, people talking all around you, but then your name and flight number is announced, and all of a sudden you think, *Wait, that was my name.* That's your RAS at work. Your subconscious screens out things you determine aren't important, and it alerts you to things you think are important.

I never fully believed this until my first child was born. I used to be able to sleep through anything—and I mean virtually anything. Once an automobile accident happened in front of my home. Police and ambulance sirens, neighbors, and multitudes of people were outside my front door. I'm told the noise was deafening. I don't know because I slept through it all! I discovered it the next morning when I walked out my front door to find police tape across the walkway! Like I said, I could sleep through almost anything.

A few years later, I was about to welcome my first child into the world, and I was worried—really worried. What if she woke up at night crying, and I didn't hear her? That would be terrible. I went to bed the first night really concerned about that. Around 2:00 a.m., I sat straight up in bed and realized that my daughter was whimpering (not even crying loudly). I immediately nudged my wife and said, "Honey, I think the baby's awake." (I know—women everywhere hate me now. Sorry.) But forget about the lousy-husband issue, and think about the power of the RAS. It's incredible. I could sleep through an automobile accident outside my front door, but I woke up with the slight cries of a baby. Our Reticular Activating System is amazingly powerful.

Our RAS has that same power as it relates to referrals. We are all standing in the middle of referrals every day. They are all around us. We simply need to put our RAS to work to hear them. For that to happen, we need to start by listening for the "language of referrals." Whenever anyone says to you, "I can't..." "I need..." "I want..." or "I don't know..." whatever they say next is most likely a referral for someone! These phrases (along with many others) indicate that the person talking needs something. That something they need is a possible referral you can give. If you train your RAS to open its filter and recognize those phrases, you will almost immediately increase the number of referrals you can give to your referral partners.

Giving referrals is one of the best ways to start getting referrals. Giving referrals begins with opening your mind or Reticular Activating System to hearing all the referrals that are all around you each and every day. When you begin to do that, a whole new world of doing business opens up to you.

CHAPTER 20

Fishing for Referrals

The process of meeting people, staying in touch, and then asking for their business is a lot like fishing. If you know how to do it right, you'll regularly haul in a nice catch. If you don't know how to do it right, you'll waste time complaining that fishing doesn't work, despite the schools of fish swimming under your boat!

Do referrals happen by accident? A few years ago, a longstanding member of a business networking organization was talking about canceling his membership—not because he wasn't getting enough referrals, but because he was getting *too much* business. That's right. Despite a full year of receiving great referrals and closed business, Mike, didn't feel that networking was a viable business strategy for growing his company's sales. He felt that the business he received was based on "chance occurrences"—one person knowing another, who happened to know him—and despite the fact that the referrals kept rolling in as a result of his networking contacts, it couldn't possibly last. So he left the group to network with a different group of people, thinking that "more is better."

Even though Mike's misguided reasoning led him down the wrong road, it raises a good question, and understanding the answer could help your business. The question is simply this: Despite what appears to be the "chance" nature of networking, does it make sense to leave your established network (that is working for you) to meet different people as a consistent means of increasing your referrals?

Mike's challenge boiled down to two things: repeatability and understanding. His training told him that the way to get more business was to target a certain kind of customer by calling people from a demographics-based list. If he didn't have enough business, he needed to make more calls. How many more? Mike could figure that out, too, because the amount of business he got was directly proportional to the number of people he contacted. It was a repeatable process that he fully understood.

On the other hand, clients he got from referrals always had a meandering storyline that he couldn't see being repeated. Sally knew Jim, who ran into Sue at their sons' baseball game, who happened to be in his group and referred Mike the business. This led Mike to conclude that the results were coincidental and couldn't possibly be repeated.

Mike's reasoning wasn't entirely off track. If you focus on the *specific* people who give you a referral rather than on the *process and relationships* that allowed it to happen, then no, you can't count on the repeatability of that exact same scenario. Or to put it another way: Sally knows Jim, who runs into Sue and ultimately gives Mike a referral. That is probably never going to happen again in precisely the same way. Step back and ask, "Is it possible that somebody in my network will know someone else who's looking for my services and will then give me that referral?" Well, that's a whole other story—especially if you focus on building relationships so that there's always a "somebody."

What led Mike astray was this: he had a "selling" mentality. Cold calling is all about selling. Selling is much like hunting. If you're going deer hunting, you are very specific about your target. You carefully scout out your hunting ground, wear the right kind of camouflage, select the proper gun, and place your tree stand downwind of the clearing. The trophy buck you want to bag comes into your crosshairs. You must be impeccable with your timing if your shot is to hit the mark. If you miss, the deer will flee, and the chances of having another shot at it are close to nil. Do you see how cold calling is like that? You put in an enormous amount of time, effort, and energy to land a meeting with a particular client. You have one shot to hit your mark, and if you miss, it's back to the drawing board. The process starts all over with a new target.

Networking, on the other hand, is more akin to fishing. If you'd like to waste some serious time, consider doing this. Make your way down to your local pond every day at noon with your fishing pole and, hang out for about an hour and a half. Slap a piece of bologna on your hook, cast your line in the water, kick back, and wait. After several weeks of catching no fish, resist the temptation to tell everyone you know that fishing doesn't work.

A great fisherman knows that numerous factors play into catching fish consistently. The lake you choose, the reel you use, the bait you select, the water temperature and depth, the time of day, the time of year, and the boat you choose all have an effect on your success. And, yes, you may want to know a little about the fish you want to catch. Much the same, the best referral networkers are well prepared. They know who they want to meet, they know which relationships they need to nurture, they are prepared to talk in an engaging way about their business, and they know exactly what they need when someone asks how they can help them this week. Just like the best fisherman, these master networkers are patient, persistent, and prepared.

There's a universal law that applies to both fishing and networking: if you do the right things consistently over a period of time, success will come to you.

CHAPTER 21

Don't Keep Score

When it comes to networking and passing along referrals, it's not about who's giving what to whom. At no point in this book do we say, "For every referral you give, you can expect one in return." Nor do we say that when you hand out more referrals, other business professionals will automatically do the same. It just doesn't work that way.

Think of giving referrals in the context of the "abundance mind-set," which is the awareness that there's more than enough business to go around. If you hear of a business opportunity that would be well suited for a referral partner—not a competitor—think of it as "excess business." When you pass this kind of excess business to others in the form of a referral, you'll wind up attracting more prospects who want to work with you. There are plenty of fish in the lake! Most fishermen don't see themselves in competition with the other guy in his boat a hundred yards away in a different cove. In fact, if they pass each other on the way back to shore, they'll probably wave to each other and ask how the fish were biting on the other side of the lake.

The principle of "sowing and reaping" states that when you do good things for other people, those good things have a way of making their way back to you—often from a different person or group of people. Some of us call this "karma." Even if it seems that you're not *directly* benefiting from the referrals you are giving to others, take note of all the other business that "just happens" to come your way:

- The guy who checks out your website because a friend shared your blog post on Facebook and gives you a call
- The old prospect you haven't heard from in ages who calls out of the blue, wanting to meet for lunch
- The inactive client who suddenly wants to renew his contract with you

Even though it *seems* like happenstance, some or all of that is likely to be new business you attracted through the relationship-building process you employ. There are particular qualities you should strive to develop that will ensure that these things happen on a regular basis. We call them the keys to becoming a networking catalyst.

CHAPTER 22

Four Keys to Becoming a Networking Catalyst

Ivan

'll be the first to admit that I'm no mechanic. In fact, when I was a kid, my father (who can fix just about anything) took me out to the garage one day and said, "Son, you'd better go to college because you're never going to make a living with your hands." Well, that was great advice, Dad. And I think things have worked out pretty well for me as a result of your suggestion.

Despite my lack of skills as a mechanic, I can, however, tell you how a catalytic converter relates to networking and your business. By definition, a *catalyst* is an agent that initiates a reaction. In networking, a catalyst is someone who makes things happen. Without a catalyst, there is no spark, and not much gets done. So what does it take for you to become a catalyst for your business and your network? Four things: initiative, intention, confidence, and motivation.

1. **Initiative**. Catalytic people don't sit still—they make things happen in all aspects of their lives. As networkers, they stay alert for a problem that needs solving and then spring into action, calling on someone from their network to solve the problem. They operate with a "Get it done now" mentality.
2. **Intention**. Catalytic people operate with intent and are goal-driven. As networkers, catalytic people have both business and

networking goals. They learn the goals of others so they can help people achieve them.

3. **Confidence**. Catalytic people have confidence in themselves and in the players on their team. This helps ensure that the task at hand will be accomplished with stellar results.

4. **Motivation**. Catalytic people are not only motivated themselves, but they also spur others on to perform at their highest potential. These people encourage others to contribute, sharing their energy and excitement through their words and actions. They are motivated by personal and professional rewards that they can't wait to share with others, and they desperately want to help others succeed.

To set your network in motion toward helping your business, make it your goal to become a catalytic person. Think of your network as a row of standing dominoes. Each domino will remain standing until you act on the first domino. As a catalyst, you must tap the first domino to watch the chain reaction of tumbling dominoes. Your network is standing in place, waiting for you to set the pieces in motion.

But what if you're looking at your rows of dominos and realize that there are serious gaps that will disrupt the chain reaction? Or maybe you don't have nearly as many dominos as you thought. Even if you are a catalytic person, you first need to have a well-rounded and sufficiently populated network.

CHAPTER 23

Raising Your Social Capital

"How many people does the average person know?" This is a common question with conflicting answers, depending on whom you ask. The number seems to be increasing with the proliferation of social media. In an effort to quantify just how many people the individual across from you *really* knows (and has the ability to connect you with), let's look at a study by evolutionary psychologist, Robin Dunbar.

In a clever experiment in the 1990s, Dunbar used the annual tradition of holiday card sending in England as the measurement of how many people the average person really knew. He was curious to see not only how many people a person knew, but more importantly, just how many of those people were worthy of a card. Why was this a great measurement tool?

Think about it: if you're going to send out holiday cards, it requires the effort of gathering the addresses, writing the cards, buying the postage, and so on. Dunbar's survey determined the people in someone's life whom he or she really endeared and considered worthy of getting a card. Those who received a card represented a person's inner circle. Those who did not get a card were in the apparent outer circle. The primary finding of the study was a single factor: the number of cards each household sent out. That number was roughly 150: the Dunbar Number. Numerous studies over the years have confirmed that around 150 is the number of deep connections a person is capable of maintaining.

This survey has given us a great baseline for just how quantifiably valuable each connection we make actually is. It essentially gives a basis for social capital, which measures not just the number of relationships one possesses, but also the depth of them. Have things changed with social media? Dunbar's study was recently replicated with Facebook, and here's what was discovered. "The interesting thing is that you can have fifteen hundred friends, but when you actually look at traffic on (social media) sites, you see people maintain the same inner circle of around 150 people that we observe in the real world," Dunbar said.

Why do some people have larger amounts of social capital than others? Some individuals are simply better connected and more influential than the average person. Usually it's because these people have invested time, effort, and energy into developing relationships everywhere they go. Unless you're a famous rock star, your social capital is a direct result of the relational investments that you've made over the years. And keep in mind that 150 is the *average*—some folks may have significantly less and others significantly more. Your inner circle isn't static, either. Your acquaintances move from the outer to the inner circle as you get to know and like them better over time. You lose touch with other people for a variety of reasons, and they move from the inner to the outer circle. Be aware of this as you give and receive referrals. Referral quality will surely be higher when someone is referring you a person from their inner circle versus their outer circle.

How can you gauge someone's social capital in today's world? A well-rounded social media presence can be a good indicator of someone's social capital. The best networkers who *don't* have a social media presence are likely a few years from retirement, and they may not be great candidates for a long-term referral partner. However, just because someone has more than one thousand LinkedIn and Facebook connections doesn't necessarily make him or her an ideal referral partner.

Here are some things to look for on social media profiles: How many recommendations does he or she have? Several hundred contacts with no recommendations might indicate that their relationships are merely digital. Are all of her posts self-generated? Are there any comments on her posts?

Are his contacts mostly other salespeople, or do they also include decision makers and business owners?

Beyond social media, how does this person typically spend his or her time each week? Face-to-face relationships support online connections, not the other way around. One of Brennan's best referral partners was a payroll representative named Terry. She singlehandedly passed him four solid referrals every month, so he was always searching for ways to reciprocate. Terry was strong in the following three categories, and these are what to look for in making your referral connections:

1. How many people know Terry? Terry would have blown way past the Dunbar average.
2. How many years has she been in business, and how many clients does she have? Terry had been in her industry for more than ten years and had hundreds of clients.
3. How many face-to-face and phone appointments does she have per week? Two appointments per day should be the minimum. Terry had five to seven!

Just because someone is in a certain profession doesn't mean he or she is automatically a good person to add to your network. For instance, many would argue that a Certified Public Accountant (CPA) is an ideal referral partner, especially if you're a financial planner or an attorney. Let's study that premise. What if he had been in business for thirty years and had hundreds of clients? Sounds like a good referral partner, right? However, what if this CPA had zero appointments per week because he has a team of bookkeepers who do his accounting for him? This gives him no connection to the very tax returns—and the people they belong to—that would uncover professional needs and allow him to pass regular and quality referrals. They say two out of three isn't bad...but in this case, it's not good.

To grow your social capital, you need to be committed to expanding and nurturing your referral relationships. However, don't make the mistake of adding people to your network *just* to make it bigger. If you do this, be prepared to pucker up and kiss a lot of frogs.

CHAPTER 24

Kiss Fewer Frogs

I n generating referrals for your business, you had better spend less time with frogs and more time with princes and princesses. And let's make sure that *you* aren't a "networking frog," either! How do you become networking royalty and find other like-minded referral partners? Let me give you some telltale signs that you might be kissing a "networking frog."

- This person is always asking you for referrals, introductions, and favors but rarely reciprocates.
- This person doesn't seem to have the time to sit down and really learn about your business, goals, and ideal customers.
- This person takes *forever* to return your phone calls and e-mails.
- This person rarely goes out of his way to help you and seems inconvenienced when complying with your request for help making a connection.
- This person talks excessively about herself and her business. She rarely asks you questions. If she does ask, she really doesn't listen to your answers.
- At networking events, this person is "on the hunt" for new prospects, shaking hands and passing out as many business cards as humanly possible.
- You always feel a little "slimy" after an encounter with a "networking frog."

How can you be sure that you are a networking prince or princess and not a frog? The simple answer is to do the *opposite* of what the "networking frog" does! A great example of networking royalty is Jerry Arrasmith, whom we introduced earlier in the book. Jerry is always giving referrals and making introductions for his referral partners, many times before they even ask! Jerry's constantly going out of his way to help people with their businesses because he's invested the time and energy to learn what his referral partners are looking for in a potential client. When you talk to Jerry, you really feel listened to. In fact, you almost have to force him to share about his business and how you can help him! You can count on Jerry to follow up on referrals you send him in a timely manner, *and* he returns your calls and e-mails within a day or two. If you run into Jerry at a networking event, he's greeting new people with a smile, introducing them to others, and being generally helpful. After an encounter with Jerry, *you* feel like royalty! That's how to become quickly known as a networking prince or princess.

Unfortunately, you may not be able to tell if you're dealing with a frog in your first meeting with someone. It may take a little time to discover a person's true networking nature, so keep your eyes peeled for the signs above. In networking, you are going to have to kiss some frogs to find your true princes and princesses. Just make sure that you are not a networking frog! Keep a stiff upper "froggie" lip, and remember these tips when seeking networking royalty!

CHAPTER 25

Not-Working

Sitting in your car, alone, you take a deep breath and prepare to walk into the building. Business cards in hand? Yes. Best mood ever? No, not really. You get out of your car and head for the front door. You try to enter, but the door seems to be locked. *Is the event canceled?* you think. Then it hits you, the little sticker on the glass that says "Push," not "Pull." You're not feeling very smart right now, and you're not even inside yet.

The event registration table is straight ahead, so you make your way over. You sign in, pay your twenty dollars, and grab your name badge. You snicker as you realize this routine has become as familiar as the TSA security line at the airport. *At least I don't have to take my shoes off,* you think. As you shuffle down to the end, you say and hear, "Hello, hello. Hi, how are you?" And then you stop. You are past the formalities. It's only you and the large, ambiguous crowd of suits, dresses, and talking heads. Several people make that awkward, glancing eye contact with you as they continue talking in their small groups.

You feel a moment of relief as one familiar face steps out of the crowd and walks in your direction. It's that outgoing, chatty lady you've met a few times before, and you're excited that you now have someone to talk to. As she gets closer, you make eye contact and smile. Just as fast, she looks away and slides by you with an ear-piercing "Hello!" for someone else. You've just been snubbed. You then hear your name over your left shoulder.

"Hey!" a slightly familiar guy yells while you notice your name was mispronounced. "How've you been?" He moves quickly into your personal space, less than a foot away, but he does not lower his voice. As he rambles incoherently, he spits a bit of buffalo sauce on your chin. But of course, he has no clue he did it.

Making an excuse to break away from Loud Guy, you retreat to the corner of the room to stand alone with your drink and a plate of celery with ranch dressing, hoping you successfully wiped off all of Loud Guy's buffalo sauce from your chin. As if it couldn't get any worse, the announcement is made to take your seat, and you're left standing there, glancing around at the mostly full tables, trying to locate a seat.

How's this networking event going for you? Having fun yet? Before you blame the event and the people attending it, let's discover the eight reasons *it's not their fault, it's yours.*

1. **Positive mental attitude**. Do you have one? Are you feeling good about yourself, your image, your vision for your business, your message, and your language? Are you equipped for compelling conversation? Rooms of random people can be tough, so are you prepared?

2. **Will this event include your prospective target market?** Does it include some of the contact-sphere professions that can lead you to them? *Contact spheres* represent those business professionals who share the same clients but do not compete with each other. In fact, they complement each other, such as a photographer, wedding planner, and DJ. Do you know who your target market and contact-sphere professions are, and how you would recognize them?

3. **Have you come to this type of event before?** Will you go again? Attending "one-off" networking functions is like visiting random farms in your community, planting and watering a few seeds in the fields, and then never going back.

4. **Have you set a goal** for the number of people you want to meet, determined what value you can offer to them, and have a system to follow up with a select few with a plan for mutual success?

5. **Why are you alone?** Would it make sense to have a friend, or even better, one of your trained referral partners, there to help identify good conversations for you and you for them? Otherwise, aren't you face-to-face cold calling?

6. **Are you there to sell?** Do you think anyone is there to buy? Are *you* there to buy? You know that relationships take frequency, trust, and time. So are you allowing others to get to know, like, and trust you before you're trying to sell to them?

7. **Do you have a plan to act like a host, not a guest?** Acting like a host is easy. Just look for those people who look lost, and go introduce yourself with a smile. Ask them about their business and introduce them to others. Isn't that more fun than standing in the corner by yourself with a plate of celery?

8. Finally, and most importantly, **do you have a unique and interesting way of talking about yourself and your business?** Why else would someone listen to you? It's surely not just because of your profession.

Networking takes a positive attitude, a skill set, a plan, and goals. How prepared are you to navigate a room full of people? If networking is "not-working," are you willing to look in the mirror and admit that the results you aren't getting might be *your fault?*

CHAPTER 26

Be Interested, Not Interesting

Let's say you're going to your very first networking event. You walk through the door to a big room full of buzzing, networking people—where do you start? What's the first thing you should do?

Before you do anything else, really observe the room. What are you looking for? To insert yourself into a group conversation gracefully, you're looking for clusters of people who are in an "open group" formation, specifically "open twos" or "open threes." Imagine that you are looking down from above…You are searching for groups of two or three people with open body language, meaning that they are not squarely facing each other. This formation makes it easier for you to approach them and start or join a conversation.

If you observe a group of two or three individuals with their shoulders perpendicular and directly facing each other, it's harder to break into that conversation. We refer to those as "closed groups." Once you locate an open group, it's very important that you know what to say when you finally walk in there and introduce yourself. Be prepared with something interesting to talk about. Have a unique way of telling others about yourself and your business.

Knowing what to say once you've entered into a conversation with an open group is the first key to success at networking events. You want to talk about your business, but not in a way that makes people yawn. How do you become an interesting conversationalist?

All too often, people try to be interesting rather than be *interested*. As soon as you're introduced to the people in the open group, the first thing you should do is *ask them questions*. "Tell me about what you do. Oh, you're an attorney! Do you specialize in a particular field of law? Tell me more about that. Are your clients individuals or corporations? What are some of the challenges of bankruptcy law?" Get them to open up. A good networker has two ears and one mouth and uses them both proportionally!

Be interested in others. At some point, the people who will make good potential referral partners will ask you about what you do. Be sure to say something that really gets their attention—a Unique Selling Proposition (USP). One of our favorites is the Referral Institute's USP. When a Referral Institute instructor is asked what he does for a living, he says, "I help people work less, make more, and *create referrals for life*." Wouldn't that get your attention? Who wouldn't want to work less, make more money, and create referrals for life?

How can you tell if you have a good USP? There's a great technique for this. Sam Horn, author of *Got Your Attention?* and *Pop!* calls it the "eyebrow test." In conversation, if a USP is interesting and provocative, you might notice that it raises the eyebrows of the listener, suggesting he or she is intrigued by what is being shared. The raising of the eyebrows displays curiosity. That's often followed by a comment like, "That's interesting; tell me more" or "How do you do that?" This is your opportunity to go deeper into what you do. On the other hand, if a USP is not creative, and possibly even confusing, the eyebrows will actually go down, or furrow, creating a look of confusion, which is definitely not what you're looking for in a good USP.

Once you find that open group to join the conversation, remember, it's really about building relationships. The best way to do that is to be *interested* first and *interesting* second. Your USP can help you with the "being interesting" portion of your discussion. This approach will help you to get the first connection off on the right foot.

Part 2
Don't Make a Move Before Making a Plan—Recap

Takeaways

- Understand the four ways to grow your business—advertising, public relations, cold calling, and referrals—and the pros and cons of each.
- Eighty percent of sales come after at least *five impressions* or contacts with potential customers.
- Referrals are the least costly form of business growth and typically produce better long-term results.
- When you really get to know somebody, amazing things happen. Make it a goal to learn something personal about each new business contact you meet.
- Never walk into an event or enter into a business relationship without knowing what you want from it.
- Cultivating referrals takes time, patience, and a commitment to the process.
- Giving referrals is one of the best ways to start receiving referrals.
- Networking is like fishing. It requires patience.
- When it comes to networking, there is no coincidence about referrals. They're the inevitable cumulative result of the day-to-day activities of relationship building.
- The four keys to becoming a networking catalyst are initiative, intention, confidence, and motivation.
- Don't make the mistake of adding people to your network *just* to make it bigger.
- Have a unique and interesting way of telling others about yourself and your business.
- Networking takes a positive attitude, a skill set, a plan, and goals. Be interested in others, and ask them questions.

Questions to Ponder

- What blend of the four ways to grow your business will you use in the coming year? How much time, effort, and money will you spend on each?
- Like Harvey Mackay, are you taking notes while on the phone with people in your networking so you might impress them later?
- How well do you know your potential customers and referral partners? Which ones do you want to know better?
- Are you using your RAS, Reticular Activating System, to identify referrals for others?
- Are you listening for the "language of referrals" during conversations?
- Who do you want to meet, and which networking events are they likely to attend?
- How many face-to-face meetings and phone calls do you have each week?
- Who are the top 150 people in your Dunbar number?
- Are you playing "kissy face" with any networking frogs?

PART 3

Get Yourself Off Your Mind

The ability to focus completely on the other person is what sets the best networkers apart. There is no better motivator in business, and in life, than the fact that givers do, in fact, gain. This is not a new concept; it was originally stated as "Do unto others as you'd have them do unto you." *Karma* is the concept that what goes around, comes around. And Zig Ziglar told us you can have anything in life you want if you help enough other people get what they want.

Newton's third law of physics states that every action has an equal and opposite reaction, and we have found that people do, too. It's been argued that people are inherently good or inherently bad, but everyone can agree to the following: that people generally respond in kind. In other words, they return what they are given. Don't believe that? Hold a door for someone, and see what they do next. Or, cut someone off in traffic, and see what they do next. Make sense? So how do you get all the business you can handle? Help others around you get all the business they can handle. In other words, get yourself off your mind.

CHAPTER 27

Are You Building Deep Referral Relationships?

Many business professionals have surface-level referral relationships. They know just enough about a referral source's business to get by. They don't actually know much about the *person*. They tend to say vague things like, "She is really nice," "You'll like him; he's a good person," or "Well, if you just meet with her, I am sure you'll like her."

How can you figure out if you have a surface-level or a deep-referral relationship? If you know the following points about people and their businesses, you have deep referral relationships:

- You believe they're an expert in their field.
- You trust them to do a great job and take excellent care of your referred prospects.
- You have known each other for at least one year.
- You understand at least three major products or services within their business *and* feel comfortable explaining them to others.
- You know the names of their family members and have met them personally.
- You have both asked each other how you can help grow your respective businesses.
- You know at least five of their goals for the year, including personal goals and business goals.
- You could call them at ten o'clock at night if you really needed something.

- You would not feel awkward asking them for help with either a personal or business challenge.
- You enjoy the time you spend together.
- You have regular appointments scheduled, both business and personal.
- You enjoy seeing them achieve further success.
- They are "top of mind" each and every day.
- You have open, honest talks about how you can help each other more.

You may be shocked at the level of personal knowledge required for a deep referral relationship, feeling that referrals should be "all about business." It's a common misconception that your business life and your personal life should be totally separate from each other. Christine Luken, the financial lifeguard from Part 1, tells the story about the day she realized that work and fun could coexist and that her referral partners could also be her friends. Here is what she says:

> Nanette Polito, my Referral Institute instructor, had invited me to a charity event for Rob's Kids. The couple who referred me to Nanette, Glenn and Shelley Warner of GorillaMaker 3-D Printers, were also going to the event. We decided to all meet up for dinner beforehand and go together. As I was leaving the house, I kissed my husband good-bye, telling him I was going to a charity event with the goal of doing some networking. Dinner was enjoyable, as was the charity event. Glenn, Shelley, and Nanette introduced me to many of their friends who were in attendance. Several people I knew were vendors at the Rob's Kids event, so I was able to make introductions as well. When I came home later that evening, my husband asked, "So how was your 'work thing'?"

> After pausing for a few seconds, I replied, "You know what? It didn't seem like work at all. It was actually fun!" That was a huge paradigm shift because work and fun had always been two separate worlds for me. Now that I "get it," building my business with referral marketing rarely feels like work!

Christine's story is far from unique. When people begin to realize that business relationships founded on genuine friendship are both profitable and fun, their work becomes much more enjoyable. Yes, it takes an investment to develop this type of relationship, and our hope is that you'll make the effort with someone you truly enjoy and have the desire to help.

After reviewing the bullet points in this chapter, what conclusions have you come to about the depth of your current referral relationships? Are your relationships more or less in line with these points, or could they use some work? If you have some work to do, what are some of the tactics you are going to start with to deepen your relationships?

CHAPTER 28

Avoiding the Networking Disconnect

Ivan

We started the book talking about the Networking Disconnect and how people show up to events looking to sell, but that almost no one is there looking to buy. So if you don't go to a networking event looking to sell, why are you there?

You should be going to networking events to build relationships. You can do that by working your way through the VCP Process˚ (Visibility, Credibility, Profitability). The VCP Process starts with visibility—people know who you are and what you do. Over time, you move to credibility—people know who you are and what you do, *and* they know you're good at it. Only then can you eventually get to profitability—people know who you are and what you do, they know you're good at it, *and* they're willing to give you ongoing reciprocal referrals. This is a chronological process that takes place over time.

The best way to help expedite referrals is to find ways to help the people you want to work through the VCP Process with. Let me give you a great example. It was years ago in Southern California, on a beautiful sunny day, and I was attending a church event with my family. I was introduced to an important and influential businessman I had wanted to meet for a long time. Because this was more of a social environment than a business one, I started asking him questions about himself and his business. I asked specific questions about his target market and what would constitute a good referral for his company. The last question I asked was, "So, what are some of the challenges you're facing?" The amazing thing is, he opened up and told me because I had just spent time really listening to him.

"Well, you know what, Ivan, my biggest challenge is getting money to charitable organizations. My company is a very successful business now, and I really want to give more money to charity. I'm too small to have my own foundation and too big not to be doing charitable work as a company. I'm struggling with how to make that happen." So I asked, "Are you familiar with community foundations? They're all over the world."

He replied, "No, what are they?"

I said, "You can create a fund within a large charitable foundation. Even though you're not big yourself, you can be part of a big organization."

"I've never heard of that. Are you familiar with one?"

I said, "Yes, I'm active in one."

"Could you introduce me to somebody?"

There we were, at a church event. Most people would say you shouldn't network at a church event. And it's true that you should always "honor the event." So I wasn't walking around at church passing out business cards! I was simply making conversation with people. The businessman asked me, "Do you have a business card? I would love to get introduced to someone at your community foundation." I was happy to give him my card because he asked for it.

A few days later, I called him up. Did he take my call? Of course he did. I found a way to help him, and I made the introduction. If I wanted to have a one-on-one meeting with him, he would have been happy to do that. Unfortunately, we usually get this backward. We're trying to sell first—we're trying to get something—especially if we're "networking up" with someone influential. This is a big mistake and a common mistake.

Looking for ways to help people is the best way to get to credibility more quickly in the relationship process. When you've had a chance to talk to someone for a while and you ask a question like, "What are some of the challenges you're facing?" or "How can I help you?" it catches people off guard because people aren't usually asked those questions. They are used to being sold to, not helped. What's also amazing is how often people actually do come up with something when they are asked a question like that.

Relationship networking is a way of life. It's just talking to people and finding ways to help them, whether you're at church or a networking event.

The deeper you can go in those relationships, the more successful you're going to be. People will begin to view you as a problem solver and seek you out. If your network is a mile wide and an inch deep, it's not going to bear much fruit. Yes, you do need to have a broad network and meet a lot of people. Then you need to go deep with some of those people, building strong connections so you'll receive referrals on an ongoing basis.

CHAPTER 29

Don't Promise, Just Deliver

Brennan

Talk is cheap, and there's no shortage of it. Some people like to talk because they're uncomfortable with silence, others because they feel like they can't stop. Unless you are a cranky passenger on a crowded airplane or trying to read a good book at the pool, overly talkative people are usually harmless. In fact, they do much more good than harm. That is, unless their words are more than just words and are empty promises.

I have always admired those who speak less but say a lot more when they do. How do you come across? Do those around you yearn for you to open your mouth? Or do they yawn when you open your mouth? Even more important, are you viewed in your personal and professional networks as a person of actions, or merely words?

Let's take a "tough love" look at the three types of referral givers:

1. **Overpromise, underdeliver:** This is the most dangerous type of networker, especially from a credibility perspective. These folks are always are "working on something" for others, but they seldom bring any closed business to the table. While it's good to let your networking partners know you're trying to help them, it is not good to get their hopes up and then lead them down the path to nowhere. In the past eighteen years, I've watched countless referral

passers who overpromise and underdeliver. Unfortunately, they are still prevalent at networking meetings today. These people promise to make connections and introductions for you but never get around to actually doing it! They don't follow through, and they leave their referral partners hanging.

These folks have that "big hat and no cattle" persona. This person talks a good game but doesn't follow through. We think there are two reasons for that. On the one hand, some people just talk too much and never truly intend to do anything about it. However, we believe the majority of these people are anxious and they are trying to help, but they overcommit themselves. In reality, they are *not* helping because they're not following through. And then people judge them according to their behavior. They determine that the person is someone who doesn't keep his or her promises. This person offers the opportunity but drops the ball. That really hurts their credibility, and we hate to see it.

2. **Underpromise, overdeliver**: These are excellent referral partners to have in your network because they ask the right questions and often come through for you. They want the best information that only you can provide for the best way to refer you. Most conscientious networkers are in this category, me included. Those are the folks who say just enough. Let's say, for instance, that we're in a networking group together. I pull you aside after the meeting and say, "Hey, I really understand what you are looking for in a referral. However, I need a little more information. Let me see what I can do. Let me make a couple of calls. I have one person in mind who may be a good connection for you. I will keep you posted along the way because I want coaching and mentoring from you." You might say, "You know, this is how you should introduce me. I want you to use this language." I am happy to do that. I am underpromising and overdelivering while keeping you informed along the way.

3. **Don't promise, just deliver:** This is my absolute favorite! We work daily to try to become the "don't promise, just deliver" type of person. The cliché is true that "talk is cheap." When you tell people, "I can do this, and I can do that for you," be sure to deliver on your promises. The master networkers realize this truth. So they

take excellent notes about people's referral needs. They don't talk about what they are going to do because they're busy taking notes and formulating a plan of action to help you. They know their referral partners' value propositions, target markets, and how to talk about their businesses. This comes as a result of being very intimate with your team of referral partners. Then these networking masters work behind the scenes quietly and come seemingly out of nowhere with high-level referrals and ultimately closed business. The "don't promise, just deliver" networkers catch others off guard in the best possible way. They spring out of the shadows with a great referral, served up on a silver platter, the prospect ready and willing to buy your product or service. These are the best of the best, the "Networking Ninjas."

Do you deliver on your promises to your referral partners? The first step toward growth and professional development is self-awareness. Do you know how others perceive you? Here's a simple test to find out. The next time you are in a room full of people you know fairly well (not your immediate family, but not strangers), sit quietly for a few minutes and let others carry the conversation. Then, at the right time, unfold your legs, clear your throat, and lean forward as though you are about to speak. At that very second, look about the room to see how quickly everyone looks your way and how eager they appear to hear what's coming.

Did heads eagerly turn in your direction? Were those in the room hoping you'd make a comment or a contribution of some kind? Consider this the anticipation factor. This represents the number of people in the room and just how badly they're hoping you chime in. If no one notices that you were about to share your opinion, perhaps it's time to make some changes. Becoming a better referral partner begins with excellent note taking and really listening to others. Also, you need to understand the jargon that is pertinent to your referral partners so you will know what it means when you hear it. For instance, investment advisors discuss stocks, bonds, EFTs, and mutual funds. CPAs talk about C-Corps, S-Corps, 1099s, and myriad tax form numbers. In general, you should avoid using jargon so that others outside your industry aren't confused by it. However, I think it's important to know some of the jargon of your referral partners so that you know what to listen for when searching for a good referral for them. That's why the number-one step is note taking. The second change you'll need to make is having regular face-to-face talks with those in your network so that you're immersed in their business culture and language.

Our hope is for everyone to become a "Networking Ninja and to move from "Overpromise, underdeliver" to "Underpromise, overdeliver" to "Don't promise, just deliver!" We've observed plenty of people who talk a lot but don't say very much. On the other hand, we all know certain people who, every time they open their mouths to speak, automatically, everyone's heads turn, and everyone sits up and listens. These are the type of folks we're describing—those who don't promise. They just deliver. That's the person that we should all strive to be.

CHAPTER 30

Resist Coin-Operated Networking

Coin-operated networking is like a vending machine. You take some coins, stick them in the slot, push the button, and your candy bar pops out the bottom of the machine. That's transactional—and a transactional process is great for vending machines, but *not* for networking. If you're trying to network by saying, "I will give you this, now you have to give me that," you're going be sorely disappointed.

Instead, the proper mind-set is, "Let me help you out. I've got some ideas. I have a referral for you." And over time, they'll give back to you. If you try to make networking transactional instead of relational, it doesn't work because there's always a scorecard. There will always be that businessperson who doesn't get it and says, "Well, wait a minute, wait a minute. I've given you two referrals. I expect two referrals back." It may not always work that way. For one thing, the *value* of the referrals may be different. You can't simply go by the numbers—"I give you two; now you have to give me two." Two referrals to a florist are vastly different from two referrals to a real estate agent. By the same token, we don't think it's realistic to expect $1,000 worth of referral business from someone just because you passed them referrals of that amount.

If you try to make referral marketing a transactional process, it will absolutely, categorically fail. You have to enter into it understanding the whole concept of Givers Gain˚. By working with other people over time and by building relationships with them, it will come back to you.

How do you apply the Givers Gain philosophy? Here's the proper way to apply it in the beginning of a relationship with somebody. Let's say there's somebody you don't know well, but you want to know that person better and build a referral relationship. You think this person may be able to help you, and you *know* you can help him. You don't start a referral relationship by asking the person to sign a contract stating that for every referral you give him, he has to give you one in return! The way to start the process is to *give*.

The best gift you can give is a qualified referral or something else that will help a person succeed. Now, you may not want to give a referral straight out of the gate because it could hurt your reputation if something goes wrong. So before we give somebody a referral, we really get to know them first. If either of us meets someone, and they express a need or a problem that's gnawing at them, we may say, "Gee, you know, I just read an article on that very subject. Give me your business card, and I'll e-mail it to you. You might find that of value." Now, that may seem small, but now we've opened the door to deepening that connection because we've taken the time to help that person. Using this approach, you've haven't asked them for anything, other than their business card! Instead, you're giving them ideas or information that will help them in their business. In our experience, many of those people have come back later and said, "Hey, thank you so much for that article. That really helped me—it really addressed the issue. You know, I'd love to get together sometime and learn more about what you do." Now, that's the beginning of building a relationship.

The referral marketing process is much like fishing, but it can also be likened to farming. You begin by sowing seeds of helpfulness into the lives of others. It won't be long before those seeds begin to sprout and eventually blossom into fruitful relationships. It's hard to build relationships with a transactional process. If you do, you're constantly "checking the contract" to make sure that the other person is living up to the letter of the law, and that's not the way to make this work. Referral relationships require nurturing and patience.

CHAPTER 31

Referral Marketing: Know the Risks, Reap the Rewards

Ivan

During a radio interview, the host of the program asked me whether I consider referral marketing the "safest" form of advertising. Without the slightest hesitation, I confidently answered, "By all means, *no!*" He was visibly shocked by that answer. I went on to explain that I believe very strongly in the tremendous benefits that word-of-mouth marketing can bring. However, there are unique risks associated with referral marketing that aren't an issue with commercials or other forms of advertising.

When you give someone a referral, you're putting your own reputation on the line. If your referral partner does a good job, it enhances your reputation. But if he does a poor job, your reputation will likely suffer. As I said, the payoffs of referral marketing are immense—when it's done correctly. But referral marketing involves a really big risk: giving away a piece of your reputation every time you give a referral to someone. When you tell a valued customer that a friend of yours is going to take good care of her, you *must* have confidence in that friend.

But what happens if your friend lets your customer down? It comes back to haunt you. Your customer begins to lose faith in you, and because of that loss of faith, you just might lose that customer down the road. This is why it's so important to develop strong relationships with your referral partners. Once those strong connections are forged, you can rest easy, knowing that when you tell someone a business associate or a networking partner is going to take good care of him or her, that's what will happen.

CHAPTER 32

The Value of an Endorsement

Brennan

Referrals come in all forms and fashions. Introductions with endorsements are really what every referral is meant to accomplish. While this book is primarily about recommendations for products and services, one of the best referrals that can benefit your company is the recommendation for a good employee, sales associate, or partner. In fact, this is the referral that gives year after year. Nanette Polito was that referral for me.

On a snowy December evening thirteen years ago, a smiling and energetic woman walked into a holiday party I was hosting for my networking organization. I was automatically drawn to her simply because of her positive attitude. In chatting with Nanette, I quickly learned that she was a BNI member in Toledo and had recently relocated to Northern Kentucky with her husband, Joe, who worked for Toyota. She was applying for membership in a local chapter for her mortgage lending profession. She was such a believer in BNI, I knew she could be a great asset to my region. We were in need of a new BNI director at the time, so I made a call to John Meyer, the BNI director for the Toledo region. I will never forget the words he shared when I asked about Nanette: "If you don't hire her right away, you're crazy." Taking John's advice, I did just that.

Nanette went on to become a founding member of one of the largest and most successful BNI chapters in our region and in the country, with sixty members and more than $3 million in closed business annually. She started more than twenty additional BNI chapters over the next thirteen years. Most recently, she became a trainer, coach, and partner with me in Referral Institute Cincinnati. Nanette now has more than fifty Referral Institute students who invest a portion of their annual training budget to learn from her how to grow their businesses through referrals. Had we not met on that cold December evening all those years ago, none of this would have happened. If John Meyer hadn't given me that all-important recommendation, I likely would not have taken the risk. Nanette Polito, without question, is one of the best referrals I have ever received.

Unfortunately, not all referrals are this magical and life changing. There are times when a referral goes wrong. Keep in mind, there is a risk when you give or receive referrals, but then again, all of life has some degree of risk. Just because something has the potential to go wrong, that's not reason enough to avoid giving and receiving referrals. For every referral I have given or received that went poorly, there were hundreds that went great. I will take those odds any day.

CHAPTER 33

Consistency over Time Brings Trust

I t takes an investment of time and effort to build referral relationships. It's not a get-rich-quick scheme! One of the most important things we've learned is that networking is like farming. Farmers plant seeds, water and fertilize them, and patiently wait for the plants to sprout, mature, and bear fruit. Networking is about cultivating relationships with other business professionals, which takes time. In building these referral connections, the time-confidence curve comes into play. No matter what business you're in, it's going to take a certain amount of time before people have confidence in your ability to provide a quality product or service.

That's where you have to be with people in your networking group so that they can trust that you're going to do a good job. No businessperson with any sense is going to put you in front of his best client—the one who's "paying the mortgage"—or a long-time family friend unless they trust that you're going to do a good job. They don't want to risk damaging an important relationship. When you give a referral, you give a little bit of your reputation away. If you give a good referral, it enhances your reputation. If you give a bad referral, it hurts your reputation.

Is there a good way to "test the water" with a new referral partner to see if he or she is trustworthy? Try somebody out with a "low-risk referral," one that wouldn't sting too much if it goes south. If they do well, then you can give them progressively bigger and better referrals because they're building a track record of trust. Trust is absolutely critical in referrals. And how long does it take to develop trust? It certainly doesn't happen overnight!

Some professions are low-risk referrals. For example, with a florist, you can quickly and easily check out their product, customer service, and delivery. But in the case of a financial planner or a mortgage lender, if you do business with them, you're going to give them sensitive personal information. So for some professions, it takes longer for that trust to build. You're probably not going to refer that financial planner until you really, really trust her. That's why you have to view referral marketing as a long-term process. This is a way to build trust, to fill your pipeline of referrals, and it takes a while for the results to come out. But they do come out, and they come out big time! Just as a farmer is patient with his plants, you need to give your referral relationships time to develop. A farmer doesn't dig up the seeds to see how they're coming along.

CHAPTER 34

A Strikeout Can Still Be a Hit

Brennan

Salespeople have a nasty little habit of moving too quickly from prospect to prospect, from appointment to appointment. "It's a numbers game! Every *no* gets you closer to a *yes*!" Sales gurus have preached this message for decades. I get it, and of course there is *some* truth to this. However, allow me to challenge this thinking by making this statement: A strikeout with a prospect can still be a hit for your referral partners, which can lead to a home run for you! In baseball, a strikeout occurs when a batter comes to the plate, swings a wooden bat at a ball thrown by the pitcher, and then swings and misses on three attempts. This means he strikes out. He has to then take a shameful walk back to the bench and sit down until his next opportunity. In many sales environments, salespeople take the same shameful walk out the door and leave the prospect behind when they are told "no." However, when a batter hits the baseball hard enough, and it goes over the outfield wall, we call that a home run. So how can a strikeout still be a home run? Let me give you an example.

Patty was a city administrator whom I called on during my days in the insurance business. After three long months of courting her as a client, I struck out. Most salespeople would have left her far behind in their rearview mirror, but I did not. Sure, I invested three months of effort and walked away without a sale, but I managed to develop something even more valuable: a relationship. In fact, over the next several months, I went back to see Patty. But I wasn't alone—I took my referral partners with me. One of them was a payroll provider who later closed a deal with her. Next, I introduced Patty to a referral partner who sold ink cartridges to cities at 70 percent of the cost of the "big-box" office supply chains. Had I now become the guy who helped save the city thousands on toner cartridges? Yep, that's me. The next time Patty needed insurance services, who do you think she called? You guessed it: me. Have I also scored points toward future referrals from my payroll and ink-cartridge referral partners? You bet. So what at first seemed like a strikeout eventually became a home run!

Traditional sales training would tell you to leave Patty in the dust, but the best networkers realize that if you treat enough Pattys like people with needs and not closed doors, you can have dramatic success in the future. The amount of time it takes to develop a good relationship lengthens every year. Just because you don't do business with a prospect doesn't mean that relationship is not valuable. While it may not pay off for you right away, it might later. The real value of that new relationship means that your network, the one you have influence over, just expanded by one! Use this to your benefit. After all, the Givers Gain philosophy means you have to know people to give. Be sure and give the Pattys of the world the chance to be a great referral for someone else. Done right, Patty will thank you later for knowing so many great people.

Now, here comes your homework assignment. Take a look at the last ten prospects you did *not* convert to customers. Call your top three referral partners and ask them if they'd like an introduction to any of those prospects. Then set some appointments, and take the show on the road. You'll be glad you did, and so will they.

CHAPTER 35

The Willing Conversation

D o you recall ever playing with magnets when you were a child? Depending on which way you turned the magnets, they were either attracted to or repelled by one another. Perhaps, like us, it wasn't until later in life that you realized the deeper meaning behind this playful activity. This is how you might find yourself feeling, as though you are six years old again, when you make a phone call to a referral who is not a referral at all. Similar to a magnet turned the wrong direction, you are not being embraced. Rather, you are being resisted. The "warm introduction" you have been given quickly turns into a cold call. Unfortunately, little work was done on your behalf prior to this call. Let's face it: you need good referrals—people who *want* to talk to you. In other words, if you are like us, you want to offer up and receive only *willing conversations*.

Here are some tips to follow that will allow you more "willing conversations":

1. **The needs assessment.** It is *our* responsibility to be very clear and specific with our referral partners about what constitutes a good referral. This is a combination of an ideal prospect profile and the problems we are able to solve for them. For instance, our Referral Institute clients are typically small to medium-sized companies with fewer than one hundred employees. They are closely held, often family-owned, and regional with locations in three or fewer states. These companies are recognized in their communities for their investments in their employees, the local economy, its residents, and

charitable causes. Their sales associates, ten to sixty in number, are known to be highly relational. They are in a competitive industry and are committed to gaining an advantage. Their employer invests in their improvement, both financially and by allowing the necessary time for on-site and off-site training, events, and even retreats. Finally, these companies pride themselves on higher-than-average retention of their employees, due to a reputation of treating them like family.

2. **Your unique selling proposition"** (discussed earlier in the book). Do you have dozens or hundreds of competitors in your marketplace? You probably do. That means your Unique Selling Proposition, or USP, is very important because it allows you to stand out among your competition. So, what is your USP? Remember the "eyebrow test?" What are you saying that makes you stand out? What do you do that your competition cannot touch? At the very least, figure out what you do better than your rivals.

   For example, one of our niches has become the retail jewelry industry. How, and why, you might ask? For generations, retail jewelers became comfortable in their businesses and operated just as their fathers and grandfathers had before them. However, with the advent of the Internet and the emergence of national chain jewelry stores, many small and independent retail jewelers began to lose market share. So what is our USP in that industry? *We show them how they can not only compete, but gain market share by leveraging their deep roots in their communities.* That has proven to raise a few eyebrows. Since our first referral into that industry just a few short years ago, we have spoken for and worked with more than twenty jewelry associations and companies on their referral marketing campaigns. What's your Unique Selling Proposition? You'd better have more to say than just "good customer service."

3. **What's your passion? Why are you in business?** We talked about this early in the book. This is an important section. You need to go deep here and figure out your "why" if you want to truly connect with people on a personal level.

So why do you get out of bed every day? Why do you go to work? Why are you in your profession? Unfortunately, one of the most popular answers to this question is "To make money." That's the *worst* answer a salesperson or business owner can ever give! If your only goal is to make money, try your luck at the casino. How do you change lives? That's what your referral partners need to know. We have given hundreds of presentations over the years. In the beginning, many of them were for free. We enjoyed it so much, and we wanted so badly for those in our audience to walk away with something, anything, that would change their businesses, and their lives, for the better. That's all we've ever wanted. Passion is referable; we certainly hope you have some!

4. **What is your Emotionally Charged Connection (ECC)?** Big corporations spend millions on a few little catchy words. "Like a good neighbor…" "Plop, plop, fizz, fizz…" I'm sure you know the rest. Are you recognizable by more than just your smiling face? Your Emotionally Charged Connection is a phrase, leading to a story, that your referral partners can recite when referring you. If any of Brennan's referral partners bring him up in conversation, they will tell the listener, "Brennan creates referrals for life by helping people create the richest relationships of their lives. He does this in honor of, in memory of, and as a legacy to his brother, Brady, a successful businessman who passed away at the young age of thirty-two." What's your ECC? Why would anyone care? Why do you care?

Ultimately, the better the job you do of sharing these things with your network, the more likely you'll feel like the magnet that attracts instead of the magnet that repels. This will lead to more "willing conversations."

CHAPTER 36

In Networking, Person Trumps Profession

Brennan

I recently gave a presentation to members of the Independent Jewelers Organization on how to develop strategic referral partnerships. During a break, Ronnie, one of the jewelers, came up to me and said, "Brennan, I love the concept of Dr. Misner's Givers Gain, although I struggle with figuring out which professions would make good referral partners for me. The jewelry business isn't like the realtor example you gave that perfectly fits with the mortgage lender, title agent, home inspector, insurance agent, etc. Who do I look for, and how do I find them?"

Ronnie, I owe you a jewelry purchase for raising such an excellent question. For you see, in networking, you are looking for the *person* as much as the profession.

1. **The Profession.** Let's be realistic. If you are a wedding planner, you might not want to spend all your time with an estate planning attorney—unless, of course, that person is your spouse! Rather, you'll want to ask yourself, "Who shares my clients but is not my competitor?" "Who else participates in the same types of transactions as I do?" I find it interesting that Coca-Cola pays for a certain percentage of national advertising for Domino's Pizza. Why do you think that is? Because what goes great with that pizza? How about

a two-liter bottle of Coke? In choosing your referral partners, here is a checklist of what to look for:

- Do they share my target market?
- Are they conveniently located close to my business?
- Is their company established with a good reputation?
- Do they already have an affiliation with my competitor?

2. **The Person.** Once you profile the right profession and perhaps even the right company, finding the right person is everything. If you don't have the right person, the other two don't matter. Think back to high school. Do you remember the crush you had on that good-looking, funny, super-special person? His or her looks, style, and personality were just right for you. That person was your perfect match! What if you only had one date with that person? Would it mean love and happily ever after? What if you finally scored that coveted date, only to find out it was *not* a love connection, but a terrible mismatch? Although there shouldn't be any romance in your referral relationships, there had better be some chemistry. Here is a checklist of what to look for here:

- Does your potential referral partner's personality compliment yours? Different is good, as long as you appreciate their behavioral style. It's hard to be referral partners with someone who rubs you the wrong way.
- Are they ambitious and driven in their own business, taking pride in themselves and the clients they serve?
- Do they believe in Givers Gain as opposed to "Getters Gain?"
- Do they not only believe in what you sell, but are they also a fan of yours?

Imagine arriving at a tennis club on a Saturday, and you are looking for a good match with a worthy opponent. You finally find an ideal candidate, so you both agree to meet on the court in fifteen minutes. When the other person arrives, he has a golf club in his hand. This is an example of the wrong sport, or the wrong profession. Let's say you find someone who does have a tennis racket, but each time you volley, he just stands there and doesn't return the ball. That's a clear sign that you have the wrong person. For the match to be worthwhile, you need to find the right person. Ronnie the jeweler, I wish you all the best in choosing the right people, not only to play tennis with, but also to grow your business with.

CHAPTER 37

Stop Assuming, Start Asking

Brennan

The worst kinds of mind games are the ones we play with ourselves. Assumptions and self-convincing are a deadly combination for commission-based networkers.

So what is the assumption? It's that once you've developed a strong relationship with someone in your network, and reached the credibility stage, they will automatically refer business to you. And what is the self-convincing? This is the bad habit of talking yourself into the notion that business will somehow, by divine intervention, happen. That is perfectly accurate because it will happen, but only occasionally. If your business is like mine, you need regular sales, not occasional sales. This is the point when networkers begin to speak to themselves, making comments like, "Sally knows what I do, and many of her clients are in my target market. *Surely* she will think of me." Not exactly.

The book *Truth or Delusion: Busting Networking's Biggest Myth* posed the all-important question, "Can referrals be predicted?" Of course, most networkers assume that the answer is no. However, the truth is that referrals, like sales, can be predicted *if* you have a fully functioning referral marketing system in operation. This requires a strategy for identifying, equipping, and *training* a set of referral partners. Why bother? Because making sales occasionally does not get it done. We need to make sales regularly. So why do we build solid relationships that often don't bear fruit? We know it works, but we need to work it. I believe in faith, but I don't believe in telepathy. If you have earned the right to ask for some business, then stop assuming it will happen and ask for it. A good networker, at his or her core, is really just a good person. He or she seeks to understand and give. However, we can't expect our referral partners to be mind readers!

I meet weekly with a well-connected marketing consultant, Matt Plapp, in my network. Not only have we been friends for a long time, but we have also become phenomenal referral partners for each other. In fact, I became responsible for more than $100,000 of his referred business in the first twelve months of his membership in our networking group. His client list is lengthy and includes some of the premier companies in our region. One of the challenges we experienced was our jam-packed schedules, full of commitments and distractions. Given the number of e-mails, calls, and appointments Matt has daily, I cannot assume I will be top of mind for him. But because I referred him so much business, I became one of the highest-profile members of his network.

So how did I ensure that our referral relationship was a two-way street? I took the guesswork out of it for Matt. I stopped assuming and started asking. One morning, I went through my social media sites, the Internet, and even that ancient relic, the Yellow Pages, and made a list of twenty companies I'd like to do business with. At our lunch meeting that same day, before we embarked onto any other subject, I slid the list of companies across the table to him and asked, "Who on this list do you know?" Well, wouldn't you know it, he was acquainted with two of the company owners on that sheet, one of them extremely well. Matt then asked me what my goal was for meeting them, and I told him. Before we left the table, he picked up the phone and began to dial. I sat there in amazement, and amusement, as he began to brag about me and how I could help the company solve its problems. Introductions were in progress. Asking started the receiving process.

Matt is just one example. I have earned the right to stop assuming and start asking with at least seven more referral partners. Earlier, we discussed the concept of social capital, which is like an imaginary bank account between people that is composed of a series of deposits and withdrawals. The idea is that you cannot make a withdrawal from any relationship until you have made some deposits. Those who attempt to overdraw their relational accounts are really just performing face-to-face cold calling. However, an equally unfortunate scenario is when many deposits have been made on numerous occasions, but no withdrawals are made. The opportunity to make a withdrawal is there, and has been earned, but is never taken! Whatever the reason, this is like saving up a fortune over a lifetime but never spending a dime of it for your own enjoyment. Look through your connections. From whom have you earned the right to ask for returned business and introductions? Stop assuming. Start asking.

CHAPTER 38

The Law of Reciprocity Works

in Mysterious Ways

Ivan

The Law of Reciprocity is a part of Social Capital Theory, and the best way to describe it is "What goes around comes around." The premise is that, if you help other people, they will be willing to help you. It's a powerful concept, and I see it working all the time. And I'm really one of the least New Age kind of people you'll ever meet—but this works! I see folks come into networking environments who give and give and give—and it does come back around to them.

Now, sometimes it doesn't come back to them from the original person they helped. Many times it comes from a different source. So I try to tell people it may not always come back from the person they gave to, but it will come back around. The concept is that the sum of the whole is greater than the individual parts. If everyone works together and helps one another, we all benefit. You really can gain a great deal from people by giving generously to others. This is why in BNI we call it Givers Gain—if you want to increase your business and succeed, then you need to help other people. I'm sure if people just reflected on their lives and the instances when they helped someone else, they would discover it did come back to them. Sometimes, it's almost instantaneous, within an hour, a day, or a week—something major came back to them.

I think anybody who's been networking for any length of time has had this experience.

Here's a true story that happened to me. When my son was twenty, he worked part time and didn't make a lot of money. I found out that he loaned a thousand dollars to his friend. I was so ticked off! I counted to ten, trying to calm down. I'm trying to teach him to work hard and be on his own, but I'm still paying for many of his living expenses. So when I discovered that he gave a loan for a thousand bucks to some kid, I went apoplectic!

I spoke to my son, and he told me that his friend had a really serious issue—a serious problem he needed help with. And when he told me the specifics of the issue, I completely understood and said, "Oh wow!"

My son said, "That's why I gave my friend the thousand dollars. You know, we did it as a loan, but he really needs it, Dad."

Now knowing all of the facts, I replied, "I'm proud of you, son!" I'm just amazed that he would do that, and I'm sure his generosity will come back to him.

My son doesn't belong to a business networking group. He's not out there being formally taught the Law of Reciprocity. But through the example that my wife and I have given him, I'd like to think he's learned the value of giving to others. And I'm positive it will come back to him, whether through that person or someone else.

Part 3
Get Yourself Off Your Mind—Recap

Takeaways:

- It's a common misconception that your business life and your personal life should be totally separate from each other. Some of your referral relationships should go deep.
- At networking events, there's a disconnect. Most people show up wanting to sell, but nobody's there to buy. Instead of selling, your goal should be to make connections and build relationships.
- If you want people to be eager to meet with you after networking events, the key is to find ways to help them.
- It's better to underpromise—or not promise at all—and overdeliver to your referral partners. Strive to be a Networking Ninja!
- Networking is a relational process, not a transactional one. Resist the temptation to expect a referral in return for every referral you give.
- Unique risks are associated with referral marketing because you're putting your own reputation on the line. However, just because something has the potential to go wrong, that's not reason enough to avoid giving and receiving referrals.
- It takes a certain amount of time before people have confidence in your ability to provide a quality product or service. For some professions, it takes longer for that trust to build.
- A strikeout with a prospect can still be a hit for your referral partners.
- If you have earned the right to ask for some business, then stop assuming it will happen, and ask for it. Asking starts the receiving process.
- Givers Gain = if you want to increase your business and succeed, then you need to help other people.

Questions to Ponder:

- How deep are your referral partner relationships?
- How can you help your referral partners or customers this week?
- How long is the "time-confidence curve" in your line of work?
- Who are the last ten prospects who didn't turn into business for you? Would any of them be good introductions for your referral partners?
- In selecting the professions you want to work with, ask yourself these questions: "Do they share my target market? Are they conveniently located to my business? Do they have a good reputation? Are they already working with my competition?"
- In selecting the individuals you want as referral partners, ask yourself these questions: "Does their personality compliment mine? Are they goal-driven? Do they believe in Givers Gain as opposed to "Getters Gain?" Do they not only believe in what I sell, but are they also a fan of mine?"
- From whom have you earned the right to ask for referred business or introductions?

PART 4

Connect, Don't Disconnect

So far in this book, you have learned how to focus in first, how to make a plan second, and how to give third. If you stopped reading right now (please don't do this), you would likely be very successful in networking just based on these three strategies. But if you are like us, you occasionally "fall off the wagon" when it comes to doing what you know will work. It's OK; we are all human. We trip, we fall, we make mistakes, and occasionally forget the best ways to network. If you believe that what you have learned thus far will grow your business, we simply ask that you don't regress! Don't fall off that wagon. Don't disconnect.

The Networking Disconnect doesn't *just* happen when people at events are trying to sell to others who aren't there to buy. Part 4 addresses a variety of sticky situations and pitfalls that can cause beginners and experienced networkers alike to experience that disconnect. Our goal is provide you with tips to navigate these tricky circumstances and, in some cases, dish out a little bit of "tough love."

CHAPTER 39

The Three-Step Follow-Up Formula

We often see folks make the mistake of meeting numerous people at networking events, but then they don't have a system in place to follow up with the new contacts afterward. Here's the simple follow-up formula we use; it's called the "24/7/30 System."

When you meet someone at a networking event, drop them a note within the first **24 hours**. It can be a personal handwritten note or an e-mail. Use whatever approach you will do consistently.

Within **7 days**, connect with them on social media. Make a connection via LinkedIn or Facebook. Follow them on Twitter or join them on Google+. Find ways to connect and engage with them via the social media platforms you use the most. Do *not* do this as a way to sell to them; do it as a way to start establishing a meaningful connection with them.

Within **30 days**, reach out to them to set up a face-to-face meeting. If you live near each other, meet in person. If you are far away from one another, set up a meeting via Skype or by phone. At this meeting, find out more about what they do, and look for ways to help them in some way. Don't make it a sales call; make it a relationship-building opportunity.

If you use the **24/7/30 System** to follow up with people you meet, you will establish a powerful routine that will help you to make your networking efforts meaningful and successful. Use technology to help remind you to follow up at the appropriate intervals. After you send the first note or e-mail, set up reminders on your phone or calendar to follow up at one week and one month out. As the late, great motivational speaker and author Jim Rohn, used to say, "The fortune is in the follow-up."

CHAPTER 40

Communication Is Key

As important as it is to follow up with the new contacts you make, it's even *more* important to follow up and have great communication with your established referral partners. This is especially true when you're giving and receiving referrals. Communication is the key to ensuring the referral-passing process is a smooth one.

When one of your referral partners makes a connection for you, it's a good idea to keep that person apprized of your progress with that referral. It might be as easy as forwarding or copying her on an e-mail so she can see that you have an appointment booked with the potential client she sent your way. This also reminds you to thank your referral partner when the deal is closed. If something doesn't go quite right or the referral isn't ready to buy, it's extremely important that you let the person who passed you the referral know this information. It may be a "teachable moment" for you to explain why this person really wasn't an ideal referral or to clear up any misunderstandings.

If you are the one passing the referral to someone in your network, you should check back with her periodically to see how things are going. Maybe there is something more you can do to "warm the referral up" a bit so that your referral partner has an easier time making the connection. Instead of just passing out her business card, you could facilitate a lunch meeting and personally introduce your referral partner to the person you know who needs her product or service. Once business has transpired, it's smart to call your friend and make sure the transaction was a good one for her. If not, find out why and see what you can do to remedy the situation.

You might think this is a lot of following up to do, and you're not entirely wrong. However, if a referral "goes south" and you don't communicate with your referral partner about the situation, you're going to have a mess on your hands. We've found it's always best to overcommunicate a little bit to avoid misunderstanding and hurt feelings.

CHAPTER 41

Are You Unintentionally Abusing

Your Relationships?

Ivan

One of the worst faux pas I've seen in business is confusing direct selling with networking. Some people assume that networking's really just about closing deals as opposed to building relationships. And there are so many things that I've seen people do wrong! The biggest mistake you can make is to abuse your networking relationships because you've invested a good deal of time and effort into them. You have someone that you can call on because you've invested—and they've invested in you. So the last thing you want to do is abuse those relationships.

The most glaring example I've ever seen was a woman who invited her personal network to her "birthday party." She said, "It's my fiftieth party. I'd love to have my close business associates and friends come and celebrate." One woman who was invited told me she went to the "party," and it turned out to be a sales pitch—not a party at all! When the woman arrived, she walked through the door, and a sizeable group of people was sitting in a great big semicircle in the living room. A guy standing up there with a flip chart, doing a business-opportunity presentation. The woman who attended was saying to herself, "What? I thought this was a birthday party!" But it wasn't a birthday party at all; it was a business pitch! To top it off, the woman went there hungry, expecting there to be snacks and, of course, a birthday cake. No! You know what they had for refreshments? The diet shake from that multilevel marketing company—that was it. Essentially, her associate deceived her into coming to a business presentation under the guise of a birthday party, so you can understand why this abuse of trust basically ended the relationship. The woman told me, "I felt so used in that relationship."

When you're starting out building your networking relationships, be wary of making the following mistakes: not following up, confusing direct selling with networking, premature solicitation, and abusing the relationship. By the way, we don't network perfectly in the beginning. I didn't know what I was doing when I started networking. I was trying to close deals too soon and I couldn't figure out why people didn't want to talk to me again. I had to learn how to do this. We all have to learn. The more we can recognize what we've done wrong and learn from that, the more successful we're going to be.

CHAPTER 42

The Teacher Was Wrong;

Name Calling Is a Must

Brennan

As a younger man, I have fond memories of conversations I had with my older brother. He was successful in business and had many friends. Knowing this, I always paid close attention to what he had to say. On a car ride to lunch one day, he shared with me one of his pet peeves: being called "guy"—as in, "Hey, there, guy" or "What do you say, guy?" I found that interesting because being called "guy" did not offend me. In fact, I brainstormed all the "I don't know your name clichés," including chief, sport, fella, partner, buddy, boss, pal, and of course, guy. None of these bothered me, so why was my brother offended by the term "guy"? As I got older, I realized that it was not the word "guy" that was offensive; it was the arrogance and/or laziness of the folks who use and abuse those terms. Which is easier—learning everyone's names or picking one generic name for everyone? Why not call all men "pal" and all women "sweetie"? On to the easy life! OK, I'll stop joking around, but it's only funny because these people do exist! Now, I realize that most of us don't use these generic names; typically we just don't say anything. However, there are an elite few who regularly remember to speak the sweetest sound a human being can utter: that person's name. If you are like me, you appreciate a couple of good strategies for drawing out the precious name of the person that you may have forgotten.

First, teamwork is everything. Often, you are not alone at networking or social events. Whether you are with your spouse, a business associate, or a friend, get into the habit of helping them remember names, too. For example, let's say you and your spouse are at a party and approach a friend of yours whom your spouse has only met a few times. In the first five seconds of the greeting, politely say, "Honey, you remember Bill, don't you?" To which your spouse will proclaim, "Of course! Nice to see you again, Bill." Do this enough and your spouse, among others, will do this for you in return.

What if you're by yourself and don't remember the other person's name? How do you proceed from there? You could hang out in the corner, hoping not to make eye contact. But now you've added insult to injury by not only forgetting their name, but you are also snubbing them, too! Here's a good alternative. With all the confidence in the world, walk directly up to the individual whose name you've forgotten, extend for the handshake, and with your free hand, point directly back at yourself and utter the sweetest sound in your universe—your name. Then be silent. I'd love to say this happens all the time (though I cannot), but the majority of the time, that person will point at himself and do the same. Why is this a good strategy? Odds are, he has forgotten your name, too, and you've just let him off the hook.

Of course, name badges prevent the problem. Be sure to wear yours at networking events to help others avoid the embarrassment of forgetting your name! However, name badges can look a little silly if folks are wearing them at a Little League baseball game or at the swimming pool (chest hair…ouch). No matter what, people appreciate sincerity and humility. Be real and honest. If you have forgotten a name, politely ask for it again. Say something like, "I believe we've met before. I'm Brennan Scanlon. Please remind me of your name." You will lose credibility if you ask for their name every time you see them, though. If all else fails, you can always use "guy" or "sweetie"; just don't be offended if they call you "dude" or "honey"!

CHAPTER 43

How to Avoid Embarrassment when You

Can't Remember Someone's Name

Ivan

What do you do when you meet someone and you cannot remember his or her name? Yikes! That can be embarrassing. A while back, I had a chef send me a question. He said, "Look, I was in a store recently when a person yelled out to me, 'Hi, Chef! How are you?'" I faced the person and drew a complete blank. Not only did I not know this person's name, I didn't recognize him at all. I smiled and said, 'Hi, I'm fine' and kept going."

The chef said he was really disappointed with his reaction. He could have stopped and engaged in some conversation and faked it. He could have talked to him a little bit, hoping to get a clue as to how he knew the person. Certainly, the chef could have come right out and said, "Hey, I'm sorry, I can't remember your name." Or, "I'm sorry. I don't remember how we know each other." So the chef wanted to know what I would do in that situation.

Clearly, if something like this happens to you, it's important that you do what feels comfortable to you. Because I'm in the public eye as a speaker, I meet *a lot* of people, and it's not always easy to remember every single person's name and how we met. However, I really *don't* like saying, "I'm sorry,

I can't remember your name." Or "I don't remember how we know each other." I say those things only as a last resort because I've found that certain people really take it personally that they're not remembered. Many times, as soon as you recognize who the person is, you think, *How could I not have recognized that person?* It's a common occurrence to not recognize someone right away when we see them out of context, such as seeing a lawyer in casual clothes at the baseball game or your doctor out at the shopping mall.

Here are a couple of things I would suggest. First of all, a good response in a situation like that is: "Hi, it's good to see you." Even if you don't think you've met the person, don't say "Nice to meet you," because they may point out to you that they did meet you before at a certain time—often. So just say, "Hi, good to see you," and then start a simple conversation. For example, let's take the chef in the grocery store. He could have asked the person, "So, what are you planning for your big meal?" If you can avoid admitting that you don't remember who they are, this will help you both save face. Starting a simple dialogue is a great way to shake up the gray matter in your head and remember the person's name and how you know him or her. So don't duck into the next grocery aisle with your head down to try to avoid someone! It's much worse to not be seen at all.

CHAPTER 44

Not Sorry I Missed You

Brennan

How could I be sorry? If I didn't know you were there, how would I know to apologize? Every Monday morning, thousands of businessmen and women meet at a starting line. The winner of this race will not be who can run the fastest, but rather who stands out from the crowd. Isn't that the goal in a market rich with competition? So why do most people strive to blend in? That's what we were taught as children. We were told to "Blend in, stay in line, mind your manners, don't make too much noise, keep it quiet, and mind your own business." These directions kept us out of trouble then, but they put us at risk of being overlooked and forgotten now.

A good friend of mine, trainer Francois Garon, put it this way: "We are taught in school to blend in and conform, but that also meant a loss of our originality and uniqueness. Look at the TV reality shows that give singers a shot at stardom. You will witness wonderfully talented people who sing the songs of already famous artists with remarkable accuracy, but they will not advance. They become so good at being *someone else*; the judges cannot see their unique identity. Therefore, they cannot market them." Francois was right. The only thing we really have in this world to set us apart is our originality—and how well we market it.

The three dimensions of standing out include being visible, being audible, and being silent. Let's take a look at each.

1. **Being visible**. This comes down to confidence, also known as courage or swagger. When you walk into a room, how many heads turn? Are your shoulders back and your chin up? Many people move about like they are looking for lost change. Do you smile? Are you maintaining eye contact for more than half a second? Do your eyes pan the room to be sure you connect with everyone? Are you dressed professionally and appropriately? What in your wardrobe is making you unique? Lapel pins, watches, bracelets, name badges, and tie clips are accessories that people notice, and they can enhance to your image. You don't have to be dripping in "bling." Even the smallest addition like a sharp new pair of eyeglasses can make a big difference.

2. **Being audible**. Are you loud enough? Do we have to strain to hear you? Does your voice have inflection? What are the first ten words that come out of your mouth? When you answer the question "What do you do?" is your reply consistent? Do you have an Emotionally Charged Connection? This is the signature phrase that creates butterflies in the stomach of listeners before they ask you for more. For instance, when Stephanie Potter of Rob's Kid's is asked what she does for a living, she replies, "I help kids this far from the edge (holding her index finger and thumb a centimeter apart), live to see their grandchildren." When asked how she does that, Stephanie explains that her nonprofit aids suicidal children who struggle with depression and post-traumatic stress disorder.

3. **Being silent.** Is anyone mentioning you when you are not around? Are people speaking highly of you behind your back? This is the essence of referral marketing. If your visual and audible presence is spot-on, then others will speak of you when you are not there. This is when and how referrals happen. Another great "silent" strategy is to bring a referral partner along with you when calling on a client or prospect and let *them* do the talking. Recently, I invited a dear friend and referral partner, Scott Malof with Malof & Associates CPA firm, to support me at a cocktail party because I knew I'd be

seeing an important potential client. As I suspected, when the two met, Scott raved about me as I stood silent and smiled. My favorite form of credibility building is when I am earning it without saying a word. As you might imagine, I have returned the favor for Scott many times over.

What is your strategy to become visible, audible, and then silent? A good referral marketing plan doesn't happen by accident or by luck; it's by design. You have to create it, implement it, and then be held accountable to it. Blending in might be in your favor if you were a gazelle in the middle of the African jungle. Otherwise, you had better determine a way to stand out in a positive way and take the necessary measures to do so. Until then, I'm not sorry I missed you.

CHAPTER 45

OMG, I'm an Introvert!?

Ivan

Is being extroverted a requirement for networking success? Are introverts doomed to fail at standing out in a positive way? Fortunately, you *can* succeed in referral marketing while being true to your own personality.

My wife, Beth, and I were having a relaxing dinner one night a few years ago. We were sitting around the kitchen table talking when I made an off-handed comment about being an extrovert. She looked over at me and said, "Um, honey, I hate to break it to you, but you're an introvert." I smiled and said, "Yeah, sure, I'm an introvert! Ha, ha!" She then looked at me quite earnestly and said, "No, really you're an introvert."

I protested strongly. I said, "Come on, I'm a public speaker and founder of the world's largest networking organization—I'm not an introvert! I can't be. I mean, you're joking, right?" She absolutely insisted that I was an introvert and proceeded to share with me all of my introverted tendencies. Well, I have to admit I was taken aback by this. All the examples she gave were true, but I still couldn't believe I was an introvert. On the other hand, we've been married for twenty-six years. I mean, there's a chance she might actually know me pretty well.

So off I went the next day to do some research. I did an Internet search and found a test that tells you whether you are an introvert or extrovert. Was I in for a shock! The test said that I am a "situational extrovert." It explained that I was something of a loner who was reserved around strangers but very outgoing in some situations. It was at that moment that I said, "OMG, I'm an introvert!?"

In the haze of my surprise, some very important things came into clarity for me. It struck me why I started the BNI networking organization almost three decades ago. I was naturally uncomfortable meeting new people. This approach created a "system" that enabled me to meet people in an organized, structured, networking environment that did not require me to "talk to strangers." OMG, I'm an introvert!

When I visit different BNI chapters, I ask the local director to have someone walk me around and introduce me to visitors and members so that I can connect with as many people as possible. But in reality, it's because I'm uncomfortable walking around introducing myself alone. OMG, I'm an introvert!

I realized that the whole notion of "acting like the host, not the guest" and volunteering to be the ambassador at a chamber event or the visitor host at a BNI group were all the ways I used to move around more comfortably at networking events, not just ways that I recommended for those poor introverts out there to network. OMG, I am an introvert.

Who would have thought? Well, OK, besides my lovely wife. Now more than ever, I truly believe that whether you are an introvert or an extrovert, you can be good at networking. Both styles have strengths and weaknesses. If you can find ways to enhance your strengths and minimize your weaknesses, you can be a great networker.

How about you? Are you an introvert or an extrovert, and how do you use that to your advantage in your networking?

Both introverts and extroverts can excel at networking. They simply need to focus on their strengths and manage their weaknesses. Introverts are great at listening; they just have a difficult time meeting new people.

Extroverts, on the other hand, can't shut up! They like to talk, so they are great at meeting new people. Both have strengths and weaknesses. If they learn how to leverage their strengths and bolster their weaknesses, either personality type can be proficient at networking.

CHAPTER 46

Are You Worthy?

"**W**ow, your baby sure is ugly!" When was the last time you heard someone say this? Maybe never because no one is willing to say that—out loud! How about this one? "Your clothing, marketing message, and overall business image are *not* referable." Ouch, that hurts! We occasionally think this about the people we meet, like that attorney wearing an ill-fitting suit that appears to be from the 1970s, or the HVAC guy who looks like he slept in his uniform. Before expecting others to refer business to you, have you taken a close look in the mirror?

We've seen thousands join BNI groups over the years and focus heavily on building their new network but forgetting to take a good hard look at themselves. We're challenging you to make an honest appraisal of yourself and ask, "Am I worthy of business referrals?" Here are five ways to sharpen your image, thereby increasing your referability.

1. **Define your Emotionally Charged Connection (ECC):** If you are asked seven times this week, "What do you do for a living?" do you respond with seven different variations of the answer? Human beings are creatures of habit, but somehow that doesn't apply to our marketing message. Your ECC should be both scripted and also tug at the heart strings. This combination will have lasting impressions on others and, most importantly, it's repeatable. For example, Nanette Polito, a trainer for Referral Institute Cincinnati, answers the question "What do you do for a living?" this way: "I

help small-business owners and entrepreneurs get more base hits and home runs for their businesses."

2. **Walk your talk**: Do what you say in less time than you promise. Be on time for meetings, and don't be checking your phone while others are talking to you. (If it's a temptation, leave it in the car!) If you are *not* going to do something, *don't* say you will. Follow up on everything and with everyone. What you do thunders so loudly above your head that I cannot hear the words you speak.

3. **Dress for success**: If you are a mechanic and you wear a three-piece suit to a business meeting, one might assume you're on your way from a court hearing. Whatever people in your profession typically wear—uniform, polo shirt with your business logo, or a suit and tie—just be sure to wear it well. Invest in sharp new clothing every year with impeccable fit and in colors that complement you. Tuck it in, button it up, and trim it back. People notice. Finally, if you look like you are taking the day off when you are really not, we'll assume you are casual about growing your business, too.

4. **Be self-aware**: Eighty percent of someone's perceptions of you are based on your nonverbal cues. This includes your posture, eye contact, facial expressions, mannerisms, and any verbal repetitions. People love to notice these things about you but seldom bring them to your attention. One example might be overusing a phrase when speaking, such as "Does that make sense?" Brennan was in a meeting with someone who asked him more than thirty times, "Does that make sense?" Yes, it does. This phrase can come off to listeners as though we're not smart enough to follow you. There are better ways to ask this, such as "OK so far?" or "Any questions to this point?" Many times, we are completely unaware of our verbal repetitions because we say them out of habit. Ask someone you trust if you are using any unnecessary verbal repetitions or other annoying nonverbal habits like jiggling change in your pocket or hair twirling.

5. **Keep your social media presence professional**: We like to relax and catch up with friends on Facebook and LinkedIn, just like the next guy or gal. However, it's important to that your professional image exists both offline *and* online. That's not to say you can't

have fun and share a joke or funny picture on Facebook. But do be aware that people are judging you by your online behavior. Be passionate about your beliefs, but voicing them to the masses on social media can easily backfire. Want to lose friends and alienate people? By all means, go ahead and post something controversial about politics, religion, or sex. On the other hand, be sure to let folks know you are a human being and not an unfeeling robot. Two of every three posts on your personal social media channels *should* include something about your life, family, hobbies, interests, and goals. If everything you put out there is all business, you may notice you'll have very few comments and likes on your posts.

Your baby is not ugly; it's beautiful. Your business image is not ugly; it's also beautiful and worthy of referrals. We are so often focused on the externals that we forget to reflect on ourselves. Nothing else will matter unless our personal brand and referability are in order. After all, *we* are our biggest advertisement.

Now that you're confident that your "baby" is indeed beautiful, the next step is to make sure others notice it, too.

CHAPTER 47

Ignoring You Is Easy

Brennan

While at a recent speaking engagement in Las Vegas, I stayed at the MGM Grand Hotel & Casino. Every evening when I returned to my hotel room, I entered a wonderfully clean room with pleasant touches from the maid service, like my clothes folded on the bed, toiletries organized on the sink, and the sheets turned down with a mint on the pillow. During my stay, I remembered to tip my taxi drivers, my bellman, and my blackjack dealer. However, I did not tip the maids. After all that great service, you're probably asking, "Why?" In all honesty, I forgot.

I came face-to-face with everyone I tipped but never saw the maids. Even though they did a spectacular job, I overlooked them when it came to rewarding them. It's not because I am a bad person; it's because I'm human. We are designed to empathize with and endear those who are in our direct line of sight. We rely on personal interaction as a reminder. The maid service, while magnificent, was faceless to me. People cater to us every day, and we ignore them.

In business, especially in sales, you cannot afford to be in this category of "out of sight, out of mind." Here are five ways to stay consistently visible to your customers, prospects, and referral network:

1. **E-mail**. Because e-mail is the easiest form of communication, it can also be the least effective. E-mails are quickly dismissed because they take such little effort and we receive so many of them. Most e-mails are solicitations. Don't fall into this trap of only sending out "spam." Be sure to send e-mails that offer value, and always make them as personal as possible so you don't unintentionally irritate your friends and business associates.

2. **Social media**. LinkedIn is Facebook with a tie. Whatever your pleasure, be sure to post at least three to five times a week. Moreover, only one-third of your posts on social media should be focused on business. It's possible to have hundreds of connections but no real friends. We want to know you as a person first, and then as someone who has passion, and finally you can share your profession.

3. **Phone**. Remember that your smartphone has a green talk button. Use it.

4. **Face-to-face communication**. While we continue to confine ourselves to our offices, I am reminded of Dr. Misner's appeal to us all to "not be cave dwellers." You have to eat breakfast and lunch every day, so why not do this a few times a week with a good referral partner? You can kill two birds with one stone by strategizing with your referral partner about how to help each other over a meal.

5. **Thank-you cards**. Ahh, the forgotten art of a handwritten note! Your mission, should you accept it, is to send a thank-you card after every appointment. My father's best advice on this was to place a stack of prestamped (not metered) thank-you cards in your car's glove box. Write the card immediately after your appointment, before you put the car in drive, and then find the nearest mailbox. Finally, be sure to use a pen with blue ink. Why? Handwritten notes, when written in blue ink, are difficult to duplicate when done by machine. This will show the reader that you took the time to actually write the note by hand. If hand writng is not your style, automate the process by using a service that does this for you, like Send Out Cards.

Are you easy to ignore? If so, you had better do something about it. Create a system with the options above to be sure you are not forgotten, like the maid service.

CHAPTER 48

Are You Approachable or Alienating?

Success: it's not just a word. It's also a very popular magazine you may be familiar with. The editor of *SUCCESS* Magazine, Darren Hardy, has an absolutely wonderful book that we recommend you pick up and read cover to cover. It's called *The Compound Effect*. The underlying principle Darren discusses is that "the little things add up"—which certainly applies to networking. Don't assume that because some of the strategies we outline in this book are simple and easy to understand, you shouldn't invest the time to implement them. There's a reason why we recommend that you practice some of these simple tasks on a *weekly* basis. After all, repetition produces *results*—especially when building your referral networking business.

Because the little things do add up, below are some simple things for you to consider regarding your attitude, body language, and congruence. This will help you determine whether or not people perceive *you* as approachable or alienating. The reason we believe this topic is so important is because you may be sending unconscious signals to others when you're networking that will directly affect the number of referrals you receive and the number of referral partners you make.

Approachable Behaviors:

1. **Positive attitude**—Smile, laugh, and look like you are a pleasant person to talk to. Although this seems ridiculously simple, you'd be surprised how many people forget it and therefore don't practice it.

2. **Open body language**—The book *Networking Like a Pro* introduces the reader to the dynamics of how the posture a person has when he or she stands when conversing with others. The author refers to "Open 2s" and "Open 3s." In short, if you are in a conversation with others, make sure your *open stance* allows for others who walk past you to join the conversation easily. Otherwise, they might not see you as approachable now...or ever.

3. **Congruence**—Conduct yourself as if every person you meet is the host of that particular networking event. If you were at someone's party, you'd go above and beyond the norm to make them feel good about themselves and the party...wouldn't you? You attended the networking event to make new friends and deepen relationships with people you already know, right? Then it might be appropriate to act like it.

Alienating Behaviors:

1. **Negative attitude**—No one likes a complainer! When attending networking events, please leave your own problems at the door. This is true for both your conscious signals as well as your unconscious signals. For example, rambling on about your rough personal or professional life is off-putting to a future referral partner. Listening to challenges in your marriage relationship or that your boss has favorites in the office are not the reasons why people attend networking events. If you're down, don't bring other people down. They might avoid you at the next networking event, and the next, and the next.

2. **Closed-off body language**—As just mentioned, in the discussion about Closed 2s and Closed 3s, it is possible to alienate people who might want to learn more about you at a networking function simply by standing in a "closed-off manner." Your *stance* means everything in your approachability and allows others who walk past you to join the conversation easily. If you have a scowl on your face and your arms crossed over your chest, others will likely move on to someone more welcoming.

3. **Incongruence**—Inconsistency between what you say and what you do makes a huge difference in people's perception of whether or not you are approachable or alienating. If they see regular inconsistencies, they may believe you are insincere and will regard what you say with skepticism.

So how can you be sure that people perceive *you* as approachable and not alienating? Try bringing a trusted friend or referral partner with you to your next networking event. Observe each other's body language, tone of voice, and words. Then exchange constructive feedback privately after the event, with the intent of helping each other become better networkers.

CHAPTER 49

Please Throw This Away

Brennan

Recently, I had the opportunity to speak at a meeting with more than fifty business networkers. Those in attendance each had a chance to give a very brief introduction, including their name, profession, and about fifteen seconds about their business. Several of them announced, "Be sure to take my brochure before you leave." I could not help but chuckle each time I heard that comment. After everyone was finished, I began my presentation. I felt it wasn't just a good idea, but my duty, to share with those select few who had made that announcement that no one is interested in your brochure—at least not in a first meeting. In fact, they may not even want your card. While I did get plenty of head nods from the networkers in the room who understood my reasoning, my advice must not have registered with one gentleman who, after the meeting, came up and slid his card into my hand without even saying a word. The best part: he was serious.

Perhaps there was a time when, to be successful, all one needed to do was pass out enough business cards. A popular TV commercial running right now profiles a CPA and his business cards. In it, the man states, "I carry hundreds of cards with me everywhere I go and pass them out any time I can." Although this might be excellent for the printer who supplies the business cards, it's not exactly a fun activity for the hundreds of networkers who are forced to take one. This might sound insensitive to the Type A "go-getters" who shower us with their marketing material each and every week. Here is a notion you might want to consider: *ask* if we would like one. I imagine there was a time, perhaps in the 1970s and '80s, when networking organizations promoted the shotgun approach to networking and marketing material distribution. However, I am excited to report that those days are long gone. Please allow me to cut to the chase with you by sharing what people are *really* thinking when you prematurely rush a relationship with activities like this.

1. When someone says, "I brought some brochures to pass around," what he is really saying is, "Will you please throw these away for me?"
2. When someone says, "Do you have a card?" what people often think is, *Do I really want to give it to you?*
3. When someone says in a first meeting, "Absolutely, call me this week, and we'll get together," what that often mean is, "I just made the same commitment to eight other people; you had better stay on me for four weeks, and we will eventually meet."
4. When someone says, "Great presentation!" what they mean is, "I will give you some feedback later when you ask because I don't want to hurt your feelings in front of all these people."
5. When someone says, "Sure, I know that person you want to meet. I will make the connection," what they often mean is, "You'd better make it easy on me to make this introduction. Tell me what to say. Then, make me look good. This is all assuming you have earned the right to ask me in the first place."

Even though there are always exceptions to these questions, by and large, this is what people are thinking. It's not because we are insincere or uncaring; it's just that we are overwhelmed. Don't you wish you could read minds? Unfortunately, we cannot. The best networkers take the time to read people's body language and facial expressions and ask thoughtful questions to gauge their interest. The only way to truly understand what people are thinking is to get beyond the crowd, request a one-to-one meeting, and ask them to be candid with you. For those networkers who go to a business mixer with brochures, please stop! It's the equivalent of asking someone to marry you on the first date.

CHAPTER 50

Are You a Networking Snob?

Brennan

At a recent Chamber of Commerce meeting, I was speaking to an old friend when up walked another fellow. Dressed in a nice suit, well manicured and clean-cut, he proceeded to interrupt our conversation and chat with my friend, but not with me. This fellow acted as if I had walked away, but I was still very much right there. I was taken aback because I am not completely ignored often. My friend stopped the conversation to introduce us, and I quickly looked at this gentleman and said, "You must be an important guy."

He replied, "What makes you say that?"

With a smile on my face, I paused, and then replied, "You act like it."

Caught completely off guard and with the look of sarcasm on his face, he stated, "Why would you say that?"

I replied, "Because you must be too busy to acknowledge that people were already in conversation when you stepped in."

Embarrassed, he paused, and then reached out his hand to me to introduce himself.

One thing is for certain: he will remember me in the future, especially when he sees me out networking. I wouldn't call him or others like him a "networking snob," but he risks being judged by others that way. That fellow was the kind of person who is in a hurry and only sees what he wants to see. He had a goal of talking with my friend, and nothing was going to distract him. The savvy networker certainly has a goal of meeting and talking with certain people, but she also has conditioned herself to fully survey her surroundings. She knows how to insert herself politely into a conversation already in progress. This is an important skill because it affects you everywhere.

Networking is not limited to chamber events. Any two or more people are in a social setting, it is a networking event. Unless you are a financially independent multimillionaire, you need other people to advance in life. So do you come off as a networking snob? Some people are just uncomfortable in social settings. This awkward feeling can be misconstrued as snobbish behavior. How do we overcome this hurdle? Here are three simple ways:

1. Always honor the people who are already in conversation. I have made a habit when walking into a conversation already in progress to wait for the right time to interject. If I need to get the attention of someone, I look directly at the person he is speaking to first and say, "Excuse me, please." Eye contact is a must.
2. Be aware of how you might appear. Have you ever been accused of being stuck up but know for certain you are not? It is uncanny how often shyness is misinterpreted. To overcome this perception, do everything in your power to smile and be more engaging. Ask thoughtful questions, and have a sincere interest in the response. Then offer something of value and mean it. A botanist once referred to Dale Carnegie, author of *How to Win Friends and Influence People*, as "the most interesting conversationalist." What did he do to deserve that compliment? For the better part of an hour, Mr. Carnegie *listened* to the botanist and *asked him questions*.
3. Always say good-bye to anyone you connected with. Go out of your way to do this. Compliment one thing you took away from speaking to that person. Give him or her a firm handshake and smile.

You may be thinking, *This all seems so simple.* You are right. It's common sense, but unfortunately, not common practice. The reason dogs are often treated like family is because they make us feel like we are the only ones in the world while in their presence. They are mindful of our every move paying close attention to what we say and do. We are the center of their world. Let's take a cue from "man's best friend" by making those around us feel that special, too.

CHAPTER 51

Spray and Pray Networking

Ivan

An associate of mine once told me about an interesting experience she had when she struck up a conversation with another woman at a networking function. When the woman asked my associate what she did for a living, my associate explained that she helps small-business owners build their businesses through networking and referrals. The woman smiled quite confidently and said, "I'm a business owner myself, and I'm actually really good at networking! I've been doing it for a long, long time."

This, of course, ignited my associate's interest, so she said to the woman, "I'm always interested in the tactics of successful networkers; do you mind sharing your secret with me?"

The woman flashed a self-satisfied smirk, stood up straight with an air of accomplishment, and said, "Well, I always make sure to go to networking functions with a friend and when we enter the room, we draw an imaginary line right down the middle. If my friend takes the right side, I take the left side. Once we choose the side of the room we're going to cover, we agree to meet back together at a certain time, and then we spend the entire time networking only on our individual side of the room, trying to gather as many business cards as possible. When the time comes for us to reconvene with each other, we compare how many business cards we each collected. Whoever has fewer is the loser, so that person has to buy lunch for the one who collected more."

My associate inquired further. "So what do you do with all of the business cards you gather?"

Donning her proud smile yet again, the businesswoman said, "That's the beauty of it. I enter them into my prospect list and begin to send them information about my services! Because I have all their contact information, I figure why not pitch my services to them? They're all potentially good prospects, right?"

When my associate told me this story, she was appalled that the woman would network in this way, and I wholeheartedly agree that this strategy is *not* effective. Instead, it's a classic example of how some people use networking as a "face-to-face cold-calling" technique that I like to call "spray and pray." It's basically just like taking a networking spray can (so to speak) full of meaningless information, dousing the room of people with your spray, and praying that you'll hit a few people who will respond to the generic concoction you've sprayed on them.

Networking is not...I repeat, *not*...about simply gathering contact information and spamming people at a later date. In reality, that's nothing more than glorified cold calling. *Brrrrr—it gives me the chills!* I used to teach cold-calling techniques to businesspeople many, many years ago, and although cold calling may work some of the time, I did it long enough to know that I didn't *ever* want do it again. Nearly three decades ago, I decided to devote my entire career to teaching the global business community that there is a *much* better way to build long-term business than "spraying and praying." Not only is it better, but it's also the absolute best way to grow any business. The secret to effective networking and long-term business success is investing in strong, mutually beneficial business relationships based on trust.

CHAPTER 52

Givers Gain vs. "Givers Pain"

Givers Gain is all about using the Golden Rule as a way to grow your business. We can think of no better way to spend our day than giving opportunities to others. Is it possible, though, that this giving could go wrong? You had better believe it. When giving referrals, always keep in mind the VCP Process (Visibility, Credibility, Profitability). You are in *visibility* with someone when they know who you are and recognize you at networking events. You are in *credibility* with someone when they like, respect, and trust you. You are in *profitability* with someone when you are receiving referrals, closed business, or something else of value from them. It takes time to move through the VCP Process. What's the lesson here? Practice Givers Gain only with those who have earned credibility... lest it become "Givers *Pain*."

Brennan has unfortunately had a recent encounter with "Givers Pain."

> One of my favorite pastimes, as friends and family can attest, is boating. I love spending time with my wife, Katie, and our friends and family, skimming across the lake with the sun on my face and the wind in my hair. I admit that the "unfun" part of boating is winterizing and storing my boat for the winter. As you might imagine, it can be a time-consuming endeavor, which is why I gladly pay someone else to do it for me. Recently, I asked a good friend and boat dealer whom he might recommend to have this done for me. Because he's someone I trust, I took his advice and hired

a guy I'll call Ryan to winterize my boat. Smooth as silk? Not exactly—more like rough as sandpaper. Ryan took four times longer than promised, which meant that my engine was not winterized by the first frost of winter. If you've ever owned a boat you know that this is a bad thing. He left my boat uncovered in the rain & sleet for five days soaking the interior. He left my $200 stainless-steel propeller in the back of his pickup truck and barely returned any of my phone calls. Needless to say, my friend who recommended Ryan felt terrible, and I will think twice before taking any recommendations from him in the future.

By trying to give to others and help solve problems, it's a scary side effect that you might just make things worse. Here are three ways to practice Givers Gain so that it will *not* become "Givers Pain."

1. **Understand the disclaimer**: No matter how solid the relationship you have with your referral partner is, always let the person you are referring to them know that your experience with them in the past is your best indication of how they will perform in the future. No one expects you to be a fortune teller. They, too, will be surprised if a deal goes poorly if you have shown them all the reasons this person is a good bet. Nonetheless, there are no guarantees in life; everything is a risk. We all understand that.

2. **Set the stage**: Lean positively on the relationship, and give the referral with accountability. If Brennan's friend had first made a call to Ryan and said, "I am going to send you someone who means a lot to me, and I need you to take care of him," that call could have changed everything. This also sends the message that this is a prerequisite for future referrals. This personal call should be the minimum. In Brennan's example, what if all three of them met at the boat dock to walk through the expectations as a team? Do you think the referral would have had a better outcome? Sure, this sounds like a lot of work on the part of the referral giver, but given how poorly this recommendation went, do you think he wished he would have done this? Yes.

3. **Realize that time always proves worth**: We have witnessed thousands of visitors attending BNI meetings over the years, and we're always amazed when we watch veteran members pass immediate referrals to first-time guests, and vice versa. We often learn later that deals went poorly or someone never followed up. Shocking! As humans, we have internal clocks that tell us when to eat and sleep. We also have clocks that tell us when someone has entered the credibility or trust zone. However, in haste, we sometimes forget to look at this clock. It's our opinion that six months is the minimum time frame needed to achieve solid credibility with someone.

So how do you earn the best referrals? Prove yourself over and over and over again. Then prove yourself some more.

CHAPTER 53

Why Do People Resist Networking?

W e posed that question on social media and received more than a hundred responses from people all over the world with reasons why they thought people resist the networking process. Here were the top four answers: lack of confidence, being too busy, impatience, and a general lack of understanding about the benefits of networking. Let's look at each one of these.

Lack of Confidence
A lack of confidence can manifest in multiple ways, and we're going to cover three of them in particular. The first is that some people fear not being able to contribute or reciprocate in the networking process. The second is the discomfort of meeting new people. The third is the fear of rejection.

Many times, people fear not being able to contribute in a networking environment with referrals. Although these folks may feel a bit insecure, they generally are great at networking. Why? Because they really do want to help others. If people want to network and give referrals, they tend to be concerned about being able to reciprocate and will bring value to the relationship. It's the people who *don't care* who tend not to be good at referral marketing. So if you're concerned about being able to contribute to the process of networking, you're probably going to be just fine. Hang on to that and develop relationships with people. You may be lacking in confidence when you begin the process, but you'll find that referrals will soon become a two-way street.

For some, the lack of confidence comes from nervousness at the initial thought of meeting and interacting with new people. Ivan says,

> Trust me, I can sympathize with those people! (If you don't believe me, take a look at the chapter titled "OMG, I'm an Introvert!") I discovered that I'm an introvert at heart, but in some cases I become extroverted. The experts refer to that as being a "situational extrovert." That makes sense to me because I have always felt uncomfortable meeting people for the first time in a networking environment, but once I get to know people, that nervousness goes away. I have found a great way to work around this, and I guarantee this will work for those of you with introverted tendencies. Here's what I do: I have someone who knows the majority of the people in the room walk around with me and introduce me to others. I usually ask this individual to do this in advance, especially when I know I'm going someplace where there will be a lot of unfamiliar faces. I'll meet more individuals that way, and it makes it very easy to meet new people in a networking environment. It's a great technique and works really well.

The lack of confidence can also manifest as a fear of rejection. We've all be rejected at some point in our lives. It happens—and it doesn't feel so great. We meet new people, and they don't seem very interested in us. Some will, some won't—so what? It's unrealistic to think everyone will like you. Focus on the people you can make a connection with, and practice, practice, practice. You'll find that the better you get at networking and connecting with people, the more people will want to hear what you have to say. It's all about getting out there and doing some trial and error. Work past that and you'll find that your confidence will build with experience.

Being Too Busy
"Look, I'm too busy to take on another responsibility."

"On top of everything I have to do, now I need to learn how to network, too?"

The short answer is, "Yes! You do!" If you're in business and you want your business to grow, you've got to learn how to connect effectively with people.

There are only a handful of ways you're going to effectively build your business. We do recommend that people advertise their products and services. But let us ask you a question: Have you gotten *all* the business you need from advertising? Please raise your hand if you have gotten all the business you need from the advertising you've done. (We know you're reading a book, but if it's true, raise it anyway). Hmm, we don't see any hands up. You can also build up your business using public relations. We've both had publicists for many years, and we're real believers in the power of good PR. But even a great publicist will tell you that PR isn't enough to increase the bottom line. So what else is there? Well, there's c-c-c-cold calling—which we hate! It works, but it's a ton of work, and there's a lot of rejection. Neither of us cares to cold-call ever again. There really aren't any other ways to build your business except for networking. We think networking is *much* better than cold calling!

The bottom line is this: we all have twenty-four hours in a day and seven days in a week. People find the time to do what's important to them. If people feel that they don't have the time to network or think they're too busy, it's because they don't understand how powerful it is. We hope at this point in the book, you realize that networking is the very best way to build your business. The people who don't invest the time to build their network are going to spend more money advertising, paying others to develop leads for them, or paying a publicist—again that's all fine with us! But networking is so much easier and less expensive compared to other forms of marketing.

Impatience
An independent consulting firm in the United Kingdom performed a survey regarding the amount of closed business generated in a networking environment over time. During the first twelve months, the amount of money that was generated was nothing spectacular. However, there was a sizeable jump in the amount of business that was generated in the middle

of the second year. The sales numbers climb astronomically from three to four years and from five to six years! *There is a direct and dramatic linear correlation between the amount of time spent building relationships and the amount of business generated through networking.* Yes, it takes time—it does! But the longer you stick with it, the more profitable your networking relationships will become.

Again, networking is like farming because it's about cultivating relationships with people. There is some immediate return on your networking investment in the first year of participating in any good, solid networking group. But the real rewards take longer to start rolling in. Why? Because it's about building friendships, and that takes time and *patience*. And by "time," we mean consistently investing your time, several hours, every week. The average is 6.5 hours per week...But who wants to be *average*? We recommend eight hours per week, based on another survey conducted several years ago. You can generate a ton of business by developing relationships with other business professionals. Networking is not a get-rich-quick scheme.

Lack of Understanding

Surprisingly, there's still a general lack of understanding about the benefits of networking. Some people have the misconception that networking is about selling. Many times, networking events are viewed as face-to-face cold-calling opportunities. People walk around the room saying, "Hi, my name is Bob. Let's do business, or maybe you can refer someone to me." OK, that's *not* networking—that's direct selling! We would argue that it's really bad direct selling, but it's certainly not networking. Networking is about building relationships.

One excellent response we received via social media was as follows: "Sometimes people don't realize that networking isn't something you do *to* someone. It's something you do *with* someone. It's a conversation you have. It's more listening than telling. It's about sharing and connecting with people."

A while back, Ivan heard a man at a networking training session say, "You know what I realized from this class is that it's time that I take off my bib and put on an apron." This guy was a car salesman in his early sixties, so he'd been around the block a few times.

Ivan said, "What do you mean by that?"

He said, "You know, I've spent most of my career concerned about myself—what I can "get"—and how someone can help me. I think what I've learned in this process is that I'm going to have to take off my bib and put on my apron. It's time for me to *serve others* by finding ways to help them, which will cause me to do better in return." He was right! He was absolutely right.

When people help one another, the sum of the whole is greater than the individual parts. That's the power of networking. Unfortunately, some people just don't get that, and they are leaving a lot of money on the table. But we're guessing you do get it because you're still reading this book. You're interested in learning about networking. We're here to tell you that one of the most important things we've learned in our almost fifty years of combined experience with face-to-face networking is that it's not what you know *or* who you know. You've probably heard the expression, "It's not what you know, it's who you know." Honestly, it's neither! It's *how well you know each other* that really counts. If you get that right, you'll understand the benefits of networking.

Part 4
Connect, Don't Disconnect—Recap

Takeaways:

- Use the simple follow-up formula when meeting new contacts, called the 24/7/30 System: When you meet someone at a networking event, drop them a note within the first **24 hours**. Within **7 days**, connect with them on social media. Within **30 days** reach out to them to set up a face-to-face meeting.
- Be sure to follow up and have great communication with your established referral partners, especially when you're giving and receiving referrals.
- Don't confuse direct selling with networking—they're two totally different things! Don't abuse your networking relationships.
- The sweetest sound you can utter is the other person's name, properly pronounced. Make an effort to remember other people's names.
- In order to succeed in the marketplace, you must stand out from the crowd in a positive way.
- Be sure you have a referable business image. Have something interesting to say, keep your promises, and dress the part.
- People judge you by your social media presence, so don't post anything that will tarnish your professional reputation.
- YOU are your biggest advertisement!
- In networking, the little things add up. Repetition produces results.
- Don't be a "cave dweller"! Stay consistently visible with your customers, prospects, and referral partners via e-mail, social media, phone calls, face-to-face meetings, and hand written cards.
- The best networkers take the time to read people's body language and facial expressions and ask thoughtful questions to gage their interest. Don't try to prematurely sell someone or the relationship may be over before it even starts.
- Know how to politely insert yourself into a conversation already in progress. Wait for the right time to interject.

- Don't use networking events as an opportunity to practice "spray and pray" networking, otherwise known as face-to-face cold calling. Networking is not about gathering contact information and spamming people at a later date.
- Practice Givers Gain only with those who have earned credibility...lest it become Givers *Pain*.
- Here are the main reasons people resist the networking process: lack of confidence, lack of time, lack of patience, and a lack of understanding about the benefits of networking.
- Networking's not a get-rich-quick scheme. It takes time!
- It's not what you know or who you know—it's how well you know each other that really counts.

Questions to Ponder:

- How are you going to follow up with the prospective customers you meet while networking?
- How will you follow up with your referral partners and customers when you give and receive referrals?
- Is it possible you might be abusing your networking relationships?
- What strategies are you going to use to help remember other people's names?
- How is your confidence level? Do heads turn when you walk into a room? Are you speaking clearly and loudly enough for others to hear you? Are other people speaking highly of you behind your back?
- Are you an introvert or an extrovert? What methods will you use to make it easier on yourself to meet new people?
- How referable are you? Make an honest appraisal of your attire, marketing message, and overall business image.
- Is your body language projecting a professional image? Do you have any annoying habits, such as verbal repetitions or fidgeting?
- How are you increasing your visibility with your network? Are you easy to ignore?
- Are your congruence, attitude, and body language projecting an approachable or alienating vibe?
- Are you a "networking snob"? Are you constantly interrupting others and butting in to conversations?
- Are you still resisting networking? If so, why?

PART 5

The Networking Good Life

I n the beginning of this book, we asked you to imagine a circle. This circle is symbolic of the relationships in your life. No matter what the relationship, there is a natural order to keeping it going. As you have learned, this requires a good deal of energy and planning on your end. However, if you invest this time in the right people, and in the right ways, you will enjoy amazing benefits. It will enrich your business, your cash flow, and ultimately, your life.

By now, you are aware that forming these circles does not happen in a day. It might take a year to form them, but the ongoing benefits of them can last a lifetime. As we learned in the beginning of this book, as Thomas Edison said, "Opportunity is missed by most people because it is dressed in overalls and looks like work." In the final part of this book, we have compiled real-life examples of what happens when you form those circles and then keep them going. You can—and you will—live the networking good life.

CHAPTER 54

Highly Relational Ted

Brennan

Who is "Highly Relational Ted"? He's Ted Bishop, a highly skilled auto mechanic and longtime owner of Community Auto Service. Early in my career, a good friend told me that there are really only two good connections you need in life: an attorney and an auto mechanic. Little did I know at that time just how influential an auto mechanic could be, not only in keeping my car running smoothly, but also in growing my business.

It all began more than a decade ago, when I flew on a one-way airline ticket to Atlanta, Georgia, to buy a "pre-owned" Land Rover Discovery. I quickly learned that when a car salesman sees a fresh-faced twenty-two-year-old kid come in from the airport on a one-way ticket to buy a truck, he holds all the cards. Later that day, I was driving my new-to-me Land Rover the long six-hour trek back to Greater Cincinnati. In case you were wondering about the purchase price, there was no room for negotiation.

You might think I got taken to the cleaners, and at the time, I would have agreed with you. However, the full sticker purchase of that high-maintenance vehicle would later teach me that you can't put a price tag on the value of a relationship. Ted admitted to me on my first visit to his shop that he really did not have much experience with Land Rovers. However, when I discovered the hourly labor rate charge by the Land Rover dealership, I was willing to give Ted a chance. Over the course of months and years, I became a regular customer at Community Auto Service. Some visits were quick and inexpensive, and others were not. In any case, every time I went to see Ted, he was honest with me, explained all my options, and gave me time to grieve, much like a good therapist. Even though I spent thousands, Ted saved me thousands more when compared to going to the Land Rover dealership. I could not have found a better friend, at that time in my life, given the purchase I had made. Not long after that, Ted's lot was full of Land Rovers that I had referred, not to mention additional friends and family driving other types of cars and trucks.

You might ask, how did Ted impact my life so much by just fixing my car? That's just it—that's *the least* he's done for me. Ted is more than an auto mechanic; he is one of the most endearing, highly relational friends I have acquired since getting into business. Ted taught me just how important it is to get into the personal lives of your clients, in a good way. If he wasn't riding his motorcycle in my brother Brady's memorial benefit ride, we were chatting about how much we both loved boating at Lake Cumberland. If it wasn't him sitting in the front row of one of my first speaking engagements to support me, it was when he wouldn't let me pay for an oil change and tire rotation at his shop. And if it wasn't him giving me a ride home because I was without a car, it was him liking everything I post on Facebook.

In a profession as checkered as car maintenance and repairs, I had found one of my best friends in business. Ted has accomplished this by telling his clients what he would do if he were in their shoes. He accomplished this by intentionally turning business away if a customer's vehicle did not need service. Finally, he accomplished this by knowing that if you charge a fair price and service only when needed, you will get *far* more business than you ever thought possible. In short, Ted is a great friend first, and he just happens to fix cars second. And his customers love him for that.

CHAPTER 55

Deposits before Withdrawals

Ivan

Social capital, a concept introduced in Part 2, comes as a result of building relationships. It's very much like financial capital because you have to put money in the bank before you can make a withdrawal. The same goes for social capital—you have to invest in your relationships before you ask for something in return. We live in this sound-bite society where we want everything *right now*. People aren't willing to invest time in those relationships before asking for a withdrawal, so they meet someone and want a withdrawal before they've ever deposited anything into the relationship. That's not the way to do it. It's certainly not what I teach about networking. I want to show people how to build solid relationships so that they can take a withdrawal when the time is right, without overdrawing their social capital accounts.

I have a really good friend named Alex who is in an organization with me. When I first started talking to Alex, he would offer ideas and suggestions to me without expecting anything in return. He even offered to design and build a website for me at no charge! Alex wasn't trying to sell me anything. He just kept giving me ideas and then helped with a website. Alex would connect with me every few months—in person or by phone—and he'd give me something of value. On several occasions, I asked him, "Alex, how can I help you?" I know how the Law of Reciprocity works—you have to help someone else. He would always reply, "Nothing—we're good. You know, I'm OK."

One day, Alex called me and said, "Ivan, I have a favor to ask of you."

I said, "Stop! The answer is *yes!*"

Alex laughed and said, "I haven't even told you what the favor is yet."

I replied, "Well, two things: first, I can't imagine you asking me anything I wouldn't be OK doing. I've known you long enough now that I can't imagine you would do that. The second is that you have contributed so much to our relationship. You've given and given and given—and I haven't had a chance to give back. So I'm in! What do you want?"

Alex explained to me what he wanted. He wanted me to help him promote a project. This was an easy thing for me to do. And the truth is, I would have done it for Alex even if he hadn't been so generous with me. However, because he had given so much to our relationship, I knocked myself out to make sure I gave back to him.

That's the exact opposite of what most people do. You'll really set yourself apart if, like Alex, you invest the time to build up your social capital with others. When you do finally ask them for a favor or a withdrawal, they'll be tripping over themselves to help you because you've already done so much for them.

CHAPTER 56

The Panic Room

Brennan

Living the networking good life can sometimes mean going *against* the status quo. Doug Smith, a longtime friend and twenty-five-year executive in the radio advertising industry, chose a better way to grow his business. Although Doug is an expert in that industry, he has never agreed with the traditional method of gaining new business. As a young man, he quickly learned that cold calling was *not* for him. Relationships and referrals were his go-to sales strategy. The vast majority of his industry "looked down their noses" at networking groups and events. Doug was often harassed by his coworkers for investing time in the community and people, while many of them spent time in a cold-call prospecting room in the office, affectionately referred to as "The Panic Room." Doug didn't want to be called that way and didn't want to call others that way, either. He chose another path, and he went against the radio industry's normal practices. In short, he chose a better way.

Here is Doug's approach, in his own words:

> The radio industry, like a large number of other industries, has been reliant on setting appointments via cold calls since dinosaurs roamed the earth. However, I find networking is a more reliable source for obtaining quality appointments. For years, I was a member of the Sharonville, Ohio, Chamber of Commerce. I was the

only radio sales rep I knew of in the Cincinnati market in a BNI chapter. The combination of these groups was very beneficial to my business, and the fruits of my networking labor have proven to be very successful. In an effort to create new business, my sales team was all too often instructed during two-month time periods to set one new appointment per day. How you got that appointment was up to you, as long as we each had one new appointment every day. The other members of my team relied on cold calls, while I focused on utilizing my networking community (Sharonville Chamber, BNI, Referral Institute, and LinkedIn). On one particular occasion, after eight weeks, the results were more than enough proof to me that networking was an invaluable tool to my business.

Here were the results:

Me: Seventy-eight phone calls = 70 percent of all new local business generated for the radio station over the eight weeks

The rest of the team: Average of seven hundred phone calls = 30 percent of all new local business generated over the eight weeks

The companies that became new clients of the radio station were people I had met months earlier at networking functions or through introductions via my referral partners. *It was a process, not an overnight miracle.* This seems to be the biggest stumbling block I see when it comes to business professionals not jumping into the networking world…they want immediate results. If you want immediate results, then keep cold calling because the "No" you get on the phone is definitely an immediate result. Of course there will be those people reading this who will say that cold calling must work because sales were generated over the eight weeks that were a result of cold calling, and that would be correct. But the value of networking comes in the number of calls made to generate the business. We all have the same number of hours, minutes, and seconds in a day, and it is how you spend that time that makes or breaks your business. For me, networking will always be a vital part of my day. If it's not a part of yours, I encourage you to look into it. Join a networking group, join a Chamber of Commerce, offer value to the people you meet (which is *not* collecting their business cards and then spamming them for business), help other's to grow their business, and then watch *your* business grow.

CHAPTER 57

Relationships Are Currency

How many times have you seen an entrepreneur (maybe even yourself) go to a networking event, meet a bunch of people, and then leave and never talk to them again? Too often, right? And it's not because he doesn't like them or ever want to see them again, but because he's a busy, busy person with so much going on that he can barely remember what he had for breakfast, let alone reconnect with individuals he just met.

It's a shame because these new contacts are the source of potential future business. Don't be misled. It's not the number of contacts you make that's important—it's the ones you turn into lasting relationships. There's quite a difference. Try making ten cold calls and introducing yourself. How well did that go?

Now, call five people you know well and tell them you're putting together a marketing plan for the coming year and would appreciate any help they could provide, in the form of either a referral or new business. I'll bet there are better results behind Door Number 2. Why? Because you already have a relationship with these folks, and depending on how strong they are, most of them would be glad to help you.

So here's the question: How can you deepen the relationships with people you *already know* to the point where they might be willing to help you out in the future? Here are four quick steps to get you moving in the right direction.

1. **Give your clients a personal call.** Find out how things went with the project you were involved in with their business. Ask if there's anything else you can do to help. Important: do not ask for a referral at this point.

2. **Make personal calls to all the people who have helped you or referred business to you in the past.** Ask them how things are going. Try to learn more about their current activities so you can refer business to them.

3. **Put together a "hit list" of fifty people you'd like to stay in touch with this year.** Include anyone who has sent business your way in the past twelve months (from steps 1 and 2), as well as any other prospects you've connected with recently. Send them cards on the next holiday.

4. **Two weeks after you've sent them cards, call them and see what's going on.** If they're past clients or people you've talked to before, now is the perfect time to ask for a referral. If they're prospects, perhaps you can set up an appointment to have coffee and find out if their plans might include using your services.

CHAPTER 58

How One Thank-You Card Placed

380 People in a Room

Brennan

It was a normal weekday at the office as I sifted through my mail. Not surprisingly, I received something from the Cincinnati Chamber of Commerce, our region's largest Chamber, with more than 5,500 members. As I opened the envelope, I was pleasantly surprised to find a handwritten thank-you note from the Director of Membership, John Bosse. It said, "Brennan, thanks sincerely for your membership; here's to your success." What an impact this made on me! I called John to thank him for his thank-you card. Does that seem silly? It's not. Here's why: that phone conversation turned into a lunch, which then turned into a meeting about how our two organizations might help one another. However, I knew not to rush the process because our relationship was so new. Over the next few years, I invited John and his chamber to enjoy a complimentary booth and five-minute presentation at our All Chapter BNI Awards Breakfast. What was in it for me? Nothing immediate. I was just glad to be associated with the chamber and happy to be "making deposits" with John.

After a few years of this, John and I realized that our two like-minded organizations had an opportunity to take a step forward together. Across the globe, regional networking organizations were coming together in February to celebrate networking during International Networking Week (www.

InternationalNetworkingWeek.com). Although this event is an initiative of BNI, it is open to all networking organizations, with collaboration being the mind-set. John and the leadership team at the chamber embraced the idea. What happened next? Well, 380 people gathered in a room for International Networking Week that year. The event was sponsored by thirteen different companies. It was presented by the largest chamber in our region and supported by the largest business referral organization (BNI) and the region's leader in business news. A powerful keynote speaker, Cea Cohen Elliot (www.ceaspeaks.com), changed lives that day, and 380 people then walked out of that room to change the lives of others.

Rewind a few years. Picture John Bosse is sitting at his desk at 5:48 p.m. Although John is tired and definitely ready to head home for the day, he writes out one last thank-you note: "Brennan, thanks sincerely for your membership; here's to your success." Had he walked out of the office at 5:46 p.m., there would not have been 380 people in that room, and lives would not have been changed, including my own.

Noted author and motivational speaker Zig Ziglar once said, "You don't have to be great to start, but you do have to start to be great." Life is a boomerang, so you'd better start throwing. Thanks, John.

CHAPTER 59

Diamond Quality Is Important, but

Referral Quality Is Everything

Brennan

There is an old jeweler's proverb that goes like this: "If the quality of the referral to your store is low, then the quality of the diamonds you are selling is irrelevant." All right, maybe it's not exactly a proverb, but it's the truth! It really doesn't matter what gems a jeweler is showing to a potential customer at the jewelry counter if the trust and quality have not been established with the person *behind* that counter. I've worked quite extensively with independent jewelers to help them thrive in the world of chain stores and increasing competition. The nuggets of truth I teach jewelers apply to all independent small-business owners who are in the same boat of *not* being a part of a national chain backed by a million-dollar advertising budget. Hometown, hardworking business owners deserve high-quality referrals walking in the door every day. Do you think that's achievable? Allow me to tell you two true stories.

My wife, Katie, and I married in the fall of 2009. When my friend, Tim, discovered my intent to propose, he called me and asked where I was going to buy the engagement ring. The next day, he picked me up and drove me to a jewelry shop on the west side of Cincinnati. As we drove along, Tim raved about his fantastic jeweler. By the time we arrived at the store and I was introduced, I was…dare I say…presold. I put a deposit down that very afternoon on a marvelous diamond I was positive Katie would love.

Around that same time, my good friend, Brandon, was about to propose to his fiancée, too. So how was Brandon's shopping experience compared to mine? He went to several area diamond showrooms and did not trust any of the salespeople he met. Brandon bought his diamond (gulp) on the Internet. It came in the mail, he proposed, and life was magical. Until one day soon after when his fiancée, Jennifer, was shuffling through her desk at the elementary school, only to notice that her diamond came out of its setting. After frantically searching for what seemed like hours, she finally found it on the floor of the classroom. Too nervous to mail the ring back to the online jeweler, Brandon randomly chose a jewelry store at the mall. Thirty days later, he received the diamond back, placed perfectly in the setting. There was only one little problem: his fiance Jennifer is convinced it's *not* the same diamond.

So where did Brandon go wrong? Instead of going with one jeweler he trusted, he ended up with two jewelers he did not trust. By trying to save a little money, he spent much more…not to mention the wasted time and stress. How can you ensure that you have friends like mine who put people like me in their car and drive them to *your* store or office? Here are a couple of ideas to get you started:

1. **Get out of your store, showroom, or office!** Many businesses to-day are still sitting in their offices waiting on coupon drops or ra-dio ads to drive traffic in the door. Although ad campaigns work, they will never establish the credibility and high-level referrals that *you* will. Get out of your "cave" and develop some relationships! Ideally, you should belong to three organizations. One should be a "strong contact" group that allows only one person per profession and meets on a weekly basis for the expressed purpose of passing re-ferrals, such as BNI. The second should be a casual-contact organi-zation such as your local Chamber of Commerce. These meetings happen at least monthly and are open to all professions. And third, join one social or civic organization. This could be a nonprofit or

charitable organization that will allow you to give back to the community and at the same time build some key relationships.

2. **Send a personal, handwritten thank-you card after every referral you receive.** The more of them you write, the more referrals you will get. People want to help you! Make them feel appreciated when they do so. Although you may be compelled to send a discount offer with that thank-you card, don't do it! Money is not a motivator, and it will only lessen the quality of future referrals. Send coupons or discount offers separately, but don't discount the purity of a good ol' fashioned, heartfelt "Thank you."

CHAPTER 60

Dreamers Never Dreamed

Brennan

A studious-looking older gentleman with auburn hair and a beard sits in the back of the room. With legs crossed, he listens intently, his eyes peering over his glasses as they follow me. When I look his way, I'm reminded of a university professor, the kind who wears a corduroy jacket with patches on the sleeves. About halfway through my presentation, I think, *Who is this guy?* Thankfully, I did not have to wait long; he came to me directly after my presentation had ended.

He said, "You know, I really enjoyed your talk today. I feel it is something that jewelers around the country really need to hear. We are not very good at networking and generating referrals. I am a member of IJO, the Independent Jewelers Organization, and I'm going to refer you to them to share your ideas at our national convention. Do you have a card? I will make the connection."

As one might imagine, I was skeptical but excited. Two weeks later, I was amazed to get a call from the woman in charge of booking speakers for the convention, Jennifer Herold. She asked, "Kenneth tells me you have quite a message. What is your speaking fee?" This was the first time I had ever been asked that question.

"I will get back to you very soon with that information," I replied. Little did she know, I was on Google minutes later, researching what speakers charge to present. Eight months after that phone call, I was on stage at the five-star Broadmoor Hotel in Colorado Springs in front of 350 jewelers from all over the country, and I was getting paid to be there.

Does this sound a little familiar to you? I told a small piece of this story in Part 1, but I'm going to tell you the rest of the story here to demonstrate how the compound effect of *one referral* can launch one's dream to succeed into the stratosphere. That curious gentleman in the back of the room was Kenneth Norris with Norris Jewelers in Cincinnati, Ohio. He has been in business for more than thirty years. Kenneth passed me the most exciting referral of my life. I don't believe in coincidences. Kenneth's presence was a little too appropriate that day as a prime example of Givers Gain. As it turned out, this was one of those occasions when I was reminded of the adage, "It's really not about me, is it?"

I now travel all over the country as a speaker and trainer for the Referral Institute. A vast majority of these opportunities originated from being on that stage in Colorado—thanks to that referral from Kenneth. I have shared with my audiences along the way that there are two types of people in the world: transactional and relational. The transactional people of the world see people as deals, while the relational people realize that deals come from people. Seth Shipley is a relational person. Who is Seth? Much the same way that Kenneth Norris approached me immediately after my presentation, Seth introduced himself after the speaking engagement in Colorado.

Seth remarked, "Brennan, I truly believe in the Givers Gain philosophy, and I love your ideas on a systematic approach to developing referral partners. Would you be open to speaking to our Maryland Retailers Association this fall? Also, perhaps you can give me some ideas on my referral marketing plan."

How could I say anything but yes? I was fortunate to share my message with Seth and his Maryland Retailers. But more importantly, during the preparation leading up to the conference, we grew to know each other and establish a great respect for one another through multiple phone conversations. As happens with busy professionals from different areas of the country, we lost touch for a while. Then one day I received an e-mail from one of Seth's colleagues with the subject line, "Our business has grown." The e-mail read as follows:

Hello, Mr. Scanlon,

My name is Laura Hennigan, and I'm the owner of Dreamers Travel. I wanted to reach out to you and let you know that a business associate of ours, Seth Shipley of Shipley's Diamonds and Fine Jewelry, was at one of your seminars. He did nothing but rave about you. Shipley's and Dreamers Travel have teamed up together to grow our businesses. We have an amazing working relationship and a great referral system.

We did a recent promotion that, if you spend $1,000 on a diamond, you would be entered into a drawing for a three-night and four-day all-inclusive getaway to Riviera Maya, Mexico—all expenses paid by Dreamers Travel. The drawing was held on Valentine's Day and had an amazing turnout. We continue to support each other to help grow together.

I just wanted to drop you an e-mail to let you know that you do make a difference to people. I have not seen you in person (yet), but I have been on your website, and I am very impressed. Thank you for continuing to help and educate people on how to grow their businesses. Thanks for your time, and have a great day.

Sincerely, Laura Hennigan

I could not believe my eyes! For more than a year, I had been engaged in public speaking and, to this point, I had never received an e-mail like this. I had to call Seth! I could not wait to learn what he had been doing.

Seth exclaimed, "Brennan, you would not believe it! In six months, Dreamers Travel gained more than $100,000 in new business—direct referrals from us! They've had their best off-season ever and have already hit their yearly goal. We are a major part of that because we are referring at least two people a week to them. And now, all they are working on is how they can give back to us at our jewelry store. Along with giving us free vacations that we can give away to our clients, Sandals is also giving them a yacht for a dinner cruise. Dreamers Travel is inviting us to bring our top five clients, and they will do the same. In fact, one of my top clients is becoming one of theirs. This client gave them a $250 gift card tip as a "thank you" for the excellent job they did putting together their last vacation. What's even more amazing, I have other businesses in our area calling me wanting to be a partner with us."

Seth is learning that with the process of Givers Gain and a focused approach, he is becoming the go-to person in his market. People are seeking him out and requesting to be connected with him. He has learned that, if you pass referrals openly to people in your network whom you trust, *you* will benefit the most. Sure, the referral receives good service, and the service provider obtains new business, but you create an action that will come back many times over. You are the center of the process; *you* are the connector.

Dreamers Travel never dreamed that, seemingly out of nowhere, they would have their best off-season ever. But it was no accident. If I had never met Kenneth Norris, I would have never met Seth Shipley. If I had never met Seth Shipley, Dreamers Travel would still be dreaming about how to generate some new business.

CHAPTER 61

Avoiding the Networking Disconnect–

The Three Rs to Reconnect: Coming Full Circle

This book began with the concept of a circle. That circle, a representation of the relationships in your life, mustn't be broken if they are to be successful. By reading this book, you have learned that to keep this circle going, you must first *focus in before stepping out*. This means that you have to know not only why you do what you do but also communicate that in a compelling way to your entire network, consistently. You then learned that you must *have a plan*. What good is having a compelling message if you are delivering it to the wrong audience? Then you learned that the right message and the right audience will mean very little unless you have a sincere interest in their success first. *Getting yourself off your mind* can be difficult, but it's essential if you want to inspire others to help you. Finally, you learned how to *avoid the Networking Disconnect*. This is done by watching out for the simple mistakes, networking traps, and bad habits that can potentially trip us up. If you can master closing the circle, and keep it going, all of these great relationships can continue without end.

Effective networking is a simple process: building and nurturing **relationships** in a systematic way **results** in quality **referrals** for you and your partners, and that leads to business success for all involved. Just because this process is simple and straightforward doesn't mean it is easy, though. Referral marketing is an investment of time, effort, and energy. It requires a commitment to stick with these principles, day in and day out, month in and month out, year in and year out. One thing that we both can promise you is that *if* you put in the work and have patience with the process, the harvest of referrals that comes rolling in will astound and amaze you. So when you see those people suffering from the Networking Disconnect, I hope you will invite them to lunch or coffee and share with them the secret of *relationships, referrals, and results.*

Part 5
The Networking Good Life—Recap

Takeaways

- You can't put a price tag on the value of a relationship.
- It's important to get into the personal lives of your clients in a good way.
- Build solid referral relationships by making deposits so you can take out a withdrawal when the time is right.
- Stay in touch with your referral partners, clients, and former customers to shore up your social capital with them.
- Although ad campaigns work, they will never establish the credibility and high-level referrals that *you* will.
- Send a personal handwritten thank-you card after every referral you receive. People want to help you, so make them feel appreciated when they do so.
- By using the process of Givers Gain and a focused approach, you can become the go-to person in your market.
- Building and nurturing *relationships* in a systematic way leads to quality *referrals* for you and your partners, which *results* in business success for all involved.

Questions to Ponder:

- Are you making deposits of social capital with your clients and referral partners? Who can you help today?
- How can you deepen the relationships with people you already know to the point where they might be willing to help you out in the future?
- Do you need to get out of your cave and go meet some people?
- How often are you sending handwritten thank-you cards?
- Are other people seeking you out and asking to get connected with you?
- Are you willing to make the investment of time, effort, and energy to harness the power of referral marketing?
- Will you reach out and help others suffering from the Networking Disconnect?

About the Author–Dr. Ivan Misner

Ivan Misner, PhD, is the Founder and Chief Visionary Officer of BNI, the world's largest business networking organization. Founded in 1985, BNI has thousands of chapters throughout every populated continent of the world. Each year, the organization generates millions of referrals resulting in billions of dollars' worth of business for its members.

Dr. Misner's PhD is from the University of Southern California. He's a *New York Times* best-selling author who has written twenty-one books. He is a columnist for Entrepreneur.com and Fox Business News and has taught business management at several universities throughout the United States. In addition, he is the Senior Partner for the Referral Institute, a referral training company with trainers around the world.

Called the "Father of Modern Networking" by CNN and the "Networking Guru" by *Entrepreneur* magazine, Dr. Misner is considered to be one of the world's leading experts on business networking and has been a keynote speaker for major corporations and associations throughout the world. He has been featured in the *LA Times, The Wall Street Journal,* and *The New York Times,* as well as numerous TV and radio shows and networks, including CNN, the BBC and "The Today Show" on NBC.

Dr. Misner is on the Board of Trustees for the University of LaVerne. He is also the Co-Founder of the BNI Charitable Foundation and was recently named *"Humanitarian of the Year"* by the Red Cross. He and his wife, Elisabeth, are now "empty nesters" with three adult children. Ivan is also an amateur magician and a black belt in karate.

About the Author–Brennan Scanlon

Every time a person realizes a better way of doing business—one based on relationships, trust, qualified introductions, selflessness, appreciation, and gratitude—and is willing to invest in the fundamentals of this process, this represents the moment at which Brennan Scanlon has succeeded. Brennan started his career in health insurance sales at age nineteen. He was given six employee-benefit clients worth $120,000 in annual premium. He grew that book to fifty clients worth $4.8 million in annual premium, solely by referrals.

That same year, Brennan discovered BNI when his job was to hit "play" on the VHS tape of Dr. Misner during informational meetings. Today, he is the Executive Director of forty-six BNI chapters with more than 1,100 members. Last year, these members passed 39,000 referrals that resulted in $38 million in closed business. Brennan has been an International Founders Circle Member three times and was recently appointed to BNI's International Franchise Advisory Board. He is proud to be a fifteen-year BNI member and has been thanked for more than $2 million in closed-business referrals.

Given what he learned in insurance sales and as an Executive Director for the world's largest business referral organization, Brennan has become a keynote speaker and trainer for the Referral Institute. He has presented all over the United States for Chambers of Commerce, trade associations, and various companies such as Nationwide Insurance, Edward Jones, Cincinnati Bell, US Bank, and American Family Insurance. He is an adjunct faculty member at the Carroll Community College–Miller Center for Small Business as an expert on business networking and relationship development. Brennan is a guest columnist for the *Cincinnati Business Courier*, the region's business newspaper, and was named in its 2012–2013 Class of *Forty Under 40*, which identifies Greater Cincinnati's next generation of business leaders. Brennan has a bachelor's degree in communications and marketing from Northern Kentucky University in Highland Heights, Kentucky.

The smartest decision he ever made was proposing to his wife, Katrina. Brennan and Katie were married in September 2009 and make their home in Fort Wright, Kentucky. They share a love of boating at the lake, riding their motorcycle on country roads, and traveling. Katie has a passion for photography and Brennan a passion for speaking, but most of all, their strongest passion is for one another.

BNI, the world's largest business networking and referral organization, was founded by Dr. Ivan Misner in 1985 as a way for businesspeople to generate referrals in a structured, professional environment. The organization has thousands of chapters with hundreds of thousands of members on every populated continent. Since its inception, BNI members have passed millions of referrals, generating billions of dollars in business for the participants.

The primary purpose of the organization is to pass qualified business referrals to its members. The philosophy of BNI may be summed up in two simple words: Givers Gain. If you give business to people, you will get business from them. BNI allows only one person per profession to join a chapter. The program is designed to help businesspeople develop long-term relationships, thereby creating a basis for trust and, inevitably, referrals. The mission of BNI is to help members increase their business through a structured, positive, and professional word-of-mouth program that enables them to develop long-term, meaningful relationships with quality business professionals.

To visit a chapter near you, contact BNI via e-mail at bni@bni.com, or visit www.bni.com.

REFERRAL® INSTITUTE

The Referral Institute provides the training and tools to help business professionals gain financial success through relationship-based referral marketing. Our "Referrals for Life" program is not a numbers game—it is not about spending hours making cold calls, collecting business cards, or developing a huge database of prospective customers. We don't want you to work harder to gain new business; we want you to learn how to work smarter. With the Referrals for Life® program, business referrals do not happen by accident. They result from implementing, and then consistently monitoring, a well-organized referral marketing plan.

The Referral Institute is an international franchised referral training and consulting company with locations in Australia, the Middle East, Europe, and North America. At the Referral Institute, we'll teach you how to make all your business relationships become more valuable to you and your business. As a result, you'll not only enjoy an increased quality of life because your business is flourishing, you will also gain lifelong relationships: Referrals for Life®.

If you are a motivated business professional serious about moving your business to the next level, don't wait to contact the Referral Institute headquarters nearest to you. Please go to www.referralinstitute.com to learn more about referral marketing, as well as how to attend a Referral Institute training program in your area. You may contact the organization at info@referralinstitute.com to talk about growing your business by generating qualified referrals.